Wildfire in the Wilderness

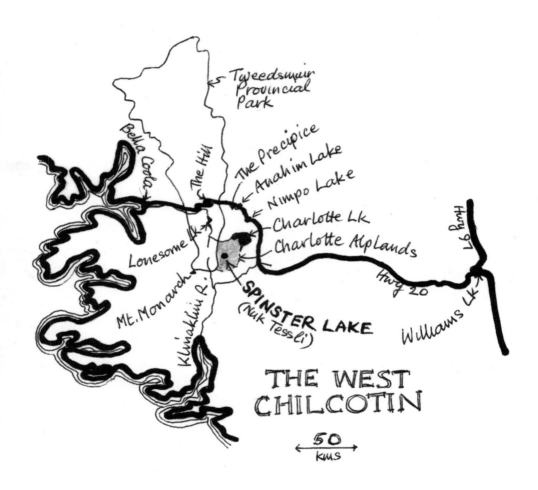

Tweedsmuir Provincial Park

Bella Coola

The Hill

The Precipice

Anahim Lake

Nimpo Lake

Charlotte Lk

Charlotte Alplands

Hwy 97

Lonesome

Mt. Monarch

Klinaklini R.

SPINSTER LAKE
(Nuk Tessli)

Hwy 20

Williams Lk

THE WEST CHILCOTIN

50
KMS

Wildfire in the Wilderness

Chris Czajkowski

HARBOUR PUBLISHING

Published by
Harbour Publishing Co. Ltd.
P.O. Box 219, Madeira Park, BC V0N 2H0
www.harbourpublishing.com

Cover design by Anna Comfort
Front cover photo by Katheryn Stewart
Printed and bound in Canada

Harbour Publishing acknowledges financial support from the Government of Canada through the Book Publishing Industry Development Program and the Canada Council for the Arts, and from the Province of British Columbia through the BC Arts Council and the Book Publishing Tax Credit.

THE CANADA COUNCIL | LE CONSEIL DES ARTS
FOR THE ARTS | DU CANADA
SINCE 1957 | DEPUIS 1957

BRITISH
COLUMBIA
ARTS COUNCIL
Supported by the Province of British Columbia

Library and Archives Canada Cataloguing in Publication

Czajkowski, Chris
    Wildfire in the wilderness / Chris Czajkowski.

ISBN 1-55017-375-8

    1. Czajkowski, Chris. 2. Outdoor life—Coast Mountains (B.C. and Alaska) 3. Fires—British Columbia—Lonesome Lake Region. I. Title.

FC3845.C56Z49 2006   796.5092   C2006-903290-4

To Rosemary and Dave Neads
Thank you

Other Books by Chris Czajkowski

Lonesome
    Memoirs of a Wilderness Dog

Snowshoes and Spotted Dick
    Letters from a Wilderness Dweller

Cabin at Singing River

Nuk Tessli
    The Life of a Wilderness Dweller

Diary of a Wilderness Dweller

To Stalk the Oomingmak
    An Artist's Arctic Journal

Acknowledgements

Thanks to the following for use of their material:

The *Great Canadian Rivers* film crew

Bruce Williams and the crew of *New Day*, New VITV (now A-Channel, Vancouver Island)

Writer Daniel Woods, Photographer Patrice Halley and the staff of *BC Magazine* (formerly *Beautiful BC*)

Rosemary Smart and staff of the *Coast Mountain News* for the excerpt in Chapter 14

Mark Hume and the *Globe and Mail* for the excerpt in Chapter 15

Rob Shaw of the *Province*

The *Vancouver Sun* for the excerpt in Chapter 19

Jeffrey Newman, webmaster extraordinaire

The staff of Harbour Publishing for taking on this book

And last but not least, my erudite editor, Mary Schendlinger, who has the most extraordinary information at her fingertips and is consequently a great pleasure to work with.

Contents

PART ONE

Spinster Lake

"Spinster" has been in use since the fourteenth century, but was not used to describe a single woman considered to be past the marrying age until the early 1600s. From December 21 in the United Kingdom it will no longer officially exist . . .

Webster's dictionary defines a spinster as "a woman of evil life and character," so it's perhaps not surprising that feminists are pleased at its abolition . . .

[Spinster] will never sound sassy or cool. Goodbye spinster, you will not be missed.

—Julie Bindel, "Death of a Spinster," *The Guardian,* 2005

The Metamorphosis of Spinster Lake

The name "Spinster Lake" was not meant to be complimentary. It was given to a remote body of water in British Columbia's Coast Mountains because an unmarried thirty-nine-year-old woman was crazy enough to think she could travel up there alone, on foot, and single-handedly build a couple of cabins along its shores. The lake was 20 kilometres beyond the nearest place to which the woman could drive a vehicle. In summer the hike to reach it would take at least two days, and in winter, on snowshoes, more like three or four. It was in a region of approximately 750 square kilometres in which all of Greater Vancouver would fit with ease, but which possessed not a single road.

At an altitude of 1,600 metres, the lake was not far below the treeline, which meant few edibles, either wild or tame, would grow. The country that surrounded the lake was worthless—the trees were trash, the fish were small. What on earth was the point? Even the First Nations people had never used the country much, although once trapping became a commercial business, a line was started by one of the Sulin family. When the crazy-woman announced her intentions, the only other human occupants were the summer guests who sporadically occupied three remote cabins belonging to resorts at the nearest settlement 40 kilometres north: the operator of a small fishing lodge whose season could not start until June, when his lake finally shed the shackles of ice; an outfitter whose clients roamed the country on horseback, and who had not a hope of covering all his territory because most of it was far too wild and rugged for these animals to negotiate; and the outfitter's guides, a couple with a boy aged six.

These last were the only real inhabitants of the area. As well as working for the outfitter, they had also taken over the trapline. They lived a nomadic existence, riding from camp to camp in the summer and going to ground in the crude, dark little trap cabins they had erected to shelter themselves in the winter. They had inherited such trails as there were from the original trapper, Sam Sulin, but kept maintenance to a minimum. Brush, swamp and inefficient gradients were of less concern to them than they would be to anyone travelling on foot, for a rider was carried high enough to be free of the scrub, and as for the unpleasant stuff going on below the horses' bellies—well, it was the horses' legs that were doing the work, not theirs. The winter snowmobile routes, which often bore no relation to the summer trails, took advantage of the many frozen lakes and calmer stretches of river, around which obstacles a hiker simply had to bush-bash through spruce swamp and windfall when the water was running free.

Because the country had been so little used, its topography was largely unnamed. The three resorts had given titles to the lakes on which they had chosen to erect their cabins, and the guide-trapper family had evolved a series of private codes to describe their wanderings, but there was little consensus among these users. "Wilderness Mountain" was one of the few official names actually marked on a map. It had been given to the highest peak in the region, which, at 2,700 metres, reared some distance above the treeline and managed to spawn a couple of glaciers. This rocky pyramid held sway over a rolling alpine plateau that was split by a river with four branches, all officially called Whitton Creek. The valleys in this watershed were clothed with a sparse forest in the biological zone known as upper montane, and they joined together and ran northwest

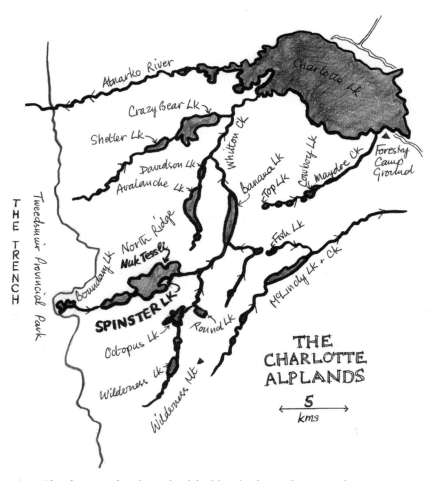

into Charlotte Lake then doubled back along the Atnarko River into the Tweedsmuir Provincial Park. There the water turned north once again and eventually reached the sea at Bella Coola. Sometime after the woman had staked her claim, the area as a whole came to be known as the Charlotte Alplands.

Trackless and wild the Charlotte Alplands might be, but it was nothing compared to the country farther west, for there was the backbone of the Coast Range, whose glacier-hung peaks as high as 4,000 metres marched along the horizon. The crazy-woman had set up camp close to the western boundary of the Alplands, giving herself a magnificent view of the mountains, but without a great deal of thought as to practicalities. You could fly to the lake by bush plane from the nearest settlement, Nimpo Lake, which was situated on Highway 20, the sparsely populated road that ran west from Williams Lake to Bella Coola. All freight would somehow have to travel that route, but to use the float plane to get those supplies from Nimpo Lake into the Alplands required money, of which this woman had very little. The building site she chose also presented many problems. The upper montane forest was too distorted and stunted to provide much in the way of cabin logs; monstrous winds battered the land; the ground on which she proposed to erect her dream was nothing more than a pile of huge boulders; there wasn't even a *beach* to land a plane on, for goodness sake (float-plane operators drool over gently shelving stretches of sand), and every aspect of the work would have to be done alone without the help of either horses or heavy machinery. What on earth could the woman be thinking of?

What is more, although she was apparently intending to start a tourist business, she had no intention of exploiting the living creatures of her surroundings and operating a hunting and fishing camp, which was where the money was at. She was one of those weird tree huggers and flower sniffers—an environmentalist, no less. Did she really expect to attract people with like-minded sentiments who were actually prepared to *walk* in there?

I am the woman who staked that claim, and nearly twenty years later I still have no other place that I call home. I do not own the property— provincial government laws prohibit the purchase of Crown land unless it has public road access. I came here simply because I wanted to live in the mountains; the government, however, would not let me occupy the land unless I had a commercial purpose, and I thought that tourism would be the answer. I considered the rolling alpine plateaus to be excellent hiking and plant-hunting country. I knew there would be little money in it: if I happened to earn some income from the business, that would be a bonus.

Placing a cabin right on the treeline would have been better from a tourism point of view, but I had to compromise and build about 300 metres below it in order to find anything resembling construction materials. It never occurred to me that the place was particularly impractical. I was already an experienced and avid hiker, had bush-bashed since I was a child, had done things on my own— spinsterishly—all my life, had grown up with wood and carpentry tools and had already built one cabin far from the nearest road about 30 kilometres north of Spinster Lake along the Atnarko River. I'd had misgivings at times, such as when I hiked in to start building— did I really think I was going to be able to move logs around this bumpy pile of boulders with only a come-along and a peavey? But it never really crossed my mind that the project was something that I would be unable to finish.

It took me three years to build the first two cabins. The bulk of the labour consisted of preparing materials and dragging them to the site. Sometimes it took all day to winch home a single log. In winter I couldn't do a lot—the snow was too deep to make dragging logs easy—and for two or three months each spring I tree-planted to earn money for the next phase of the project. I started the scheme with no spare capital at all, but every season's planting gave me just

Cabin Three

enough to pay for the summer's food, tools and supplies, and the Land Office fees.

Eight years later, I decided I needed another cabin. I had help with a lot of the heavy work for this one, and the letters I subsequently wrote to Nick Berwian, the young German carpenter who had done the bulk of the framework, became the basis of the book *Snowshoes and Spotted Dick*. As with all of the cabins, I moved in long before it was finished, cooking and carpentering in the one single room, and shaking the sawdust from my sleeping bag every night before I went to bed. Cabin Three was completed in the millennium year, and that is now my home.

I called the place Nuk Tessli, which means "West Wind" in the Carrier language, because at the end of my first summer a monstrous storm erupted hours after Cabin One's roof was finished. It came screaming down the lake from the mountains and smashed into the cabin, shaking the building with every booming roar. Trees were knocked over like ninepins and I thought the whole lot was going to blow away, roof, windows, cabin and all; Nuk Tessli, the West Wind, therefore, seemed an appropriate name for my endeavours, an apt reminder that around here, nature was boss.

The hiking business thus became The Nuk Tessli Alpine Experience. I knew there was little point in insisting upon that title for the lake, however. Most people seemed unable to pronounce it, despite the fact that I had transliterated it phonetically from the missionaries' original spelling. My own surname would be even harder for people to cope with; besides, current rules say that lakes cannot be named after people until long after they are dead. The trapping family called it Square Lake: I never did find out why, but they also called the one above it Square Lake, whereas other people often refer to that one as Cohen Lake—the trapper's own name—because his hunting clients and supplies were sometimes flown in there. Others used the name Whitton Lake for my chosen domicile—the "Whitton," for Whitton Creek, lay next to it on the map and a lot of people thought the word described the lake, but in fact Whitton Lake used to be the next one downriver, now called Banana Lake by most of the pilots because of the shape it presents when observed from above. Confusing was not the word for it. It resulted in the bizarre situation that each of the three float-plane charter companies that then operated out of Nimpo Lake referred to my lake (when they were being polite) by a different name. The charter company I used at the time, Avnorth, called it Chris's Lake; the middle one along the Nimpo Lake waterfront preferred Whitton Lake; but Tweedsmuir Air, owned and operated by Duncan and Rhonda Stewart at Stewarts Lodge, flew in the trapper's hunting clients so used the name that the trapper had invented: Square Lake. Some time during that first summer, a friend told me that "Spinster Lake" was being bandied about. I knew it was not meant to be polite, but my first reaction was to laugh. At least I was getting some recognition for my endeavours. But faced with this unwieldy nomenclature, and in view of the fact that there was no other inhabitant along its shores, I gave the stretch of water yet another designation, and simply called it "my lake."

Because of all this, I was presented with a difficulty when I had to stake my claim. I was supposed to describe the parcel of land I intended to occupy with regard to nearby surveyed features. The nearest surveyed land, however, was on the shores of Charlotte Lake 20 kilometres north. In the end I described it as: "One lake up from Banana Lake on Whitton Creek west of Charlotte Lake, on a square point of land on the north side of the lake opposite the outlet."

I figured that the story of how "Spinster Lake" evolved would be worth repeating and I wrote about it in a couple of books. It caught the imagination of a delightful person called Ruth Masters, now in her eighties and herself a lifelong spinster, who has spent much of her energetic life defending animal rights and the environment. She has a wry sense of humour and over the years she has constructed witty signs for the various protest groups that she supports. She is also a dab hand at carpentry, and has routered wooden boards to serve as signs for topographical features in the Strathcona Park and Beaufort Range near where she lives on Vancouver Island. She was so taken with the idea of "Spinster Lake" that she made a handsome

name-board for me: it now graces the waterfront and is among the first things to confront people as the plane taxis in to the wharf.

To my great surprise, a number of people have told me that they are offended by the sign. It is a shame that western cultures so readily abuse the true meanings of words. Spinsters were originally skilled people who travelled around remote British farmsteads, staying for days or even weeks, spinning the family's annual wool crop. (It takes a couple of non-stop weeks to spin two or three sweaters' worth of yarn from a single moderate-sized fleece.) Spinsters were usually women, always unattached for whatever reason (no woman with a family would be able to leave home for that length of time), and generally much looked forward to as they brought with them news from the other isolated farms. It was one of the few respectable jobs afforded a poor, uneducated woman: a spinster, therefore, was an honourable person who could maintain her independence and support herself with dignity. Insecurity, however, breeds contempt, and when people see others achieve in a field that they themselves imagine to be difficult and are ashamed of their inadequacy, the words used to describe the achiever acquire overtones of risibility. Perhaps this book will help to restore "spinster" to its true place in society.

One of Ruth Masters' crusades is naming untitled lakes, usually after those who died in World War II. She took up the cause of "Spinster Lake" with glee. But now it would appear that an official name has in fact emerged and "Whitton Lake" is what was pulled out of the hat, even though no one has any idea of where the name "Whitton" actually came from. It was once suggested to me that the creek, which runs into the previously named Charlotte Lake, was named after Charlotte Whitton, the outspoken former mayor of Ottawa, but there is no actual record of it.

Locals use their own names for the topographical features of this country, whatever the official versions might be. The float-plane companies still refer to it as Chris's Lake, Square Lake and Whitton Lake; others call it Spinster Lake, and I will continue to call it my lake until, for whatever reason, it is mine no longer.

CHAPTER 1

Louise O'Murphy

Arrived home this a.m. in Stewarts' Cessna 185. The ice went out three days ago. Nimpo Lake has been clear a month already, but up here breakup is usually three or four weeks later. Fortunately the flight-seeing tours pass overhead on their way to the Monarch Icefields and the pilots can give me an ice report.

Avnorth, the bush plane company I have used for many years, has collapsed. That leaves only one float-plane charter service at Nimpo now: Tweedsmuir Air, operating out of Stewarts Lodge. Someone is supposed to be moving onto Avnorth's old dock, but no one is sure who at the moment.

No deciduous leaves out here yet: the country is swimming in water. I can't step very far beyond the knoll on which the cabins are built without gumboots. Still a few drifts of snow in the meadow behind the cabins. The bugs were getting pretty bad at Nimpo but there won't be any here for a while. Their first major hatching occurs three or four weeks after the ice goes out. Tree swallows are finding some sort of fodder, though. They are flitting about over the lake, near the snag on the island where they always nest, and a nuthatch is giving its nasal yank yank from somewhere behind the cabin.

—Journal, June 4, 2001

I had been away from Nuk Tessli for just over two and a half months. The reason for this long absence was pecuniary, but the timing, as with all of my journeys in and out of Nuk Tessli, was dictated by the availability of aircraft and the condition of the surface of the lake.

I no longer tree-plant to support my wilderness habit. My knees rebelled some years ago and I decided to save what was left of my personal physical resources for my own mountains instead of squandering them on some hideous cutblock. The Nuk Tessli Alpine Experience has brought some increase in revenue since I began, but this has been offset by much larger demands from the British Columbia Assets and Land Corporation, which is the current title given to that official body controlling the use of Crown land. The majority of my income now comes from my writing; were I to rely solely on royalties, I would still not be able to make ends meet, but by selling the books myself I gain a much larger percentage of the revenue. To do this I rent booths in craft fairs and travel around the province giving slide shows.

I can fly home in the spring only if both the lakes are open. Pilots at Nimpo might put their floats on as early as the third week of April, but Spinster Lake may not be free of ice until late May or early June. I once tried walking home at the end of May, but the trail goes through 10 kilometres of alpine and the rotten, waist-deep snow at higher elevations drove me back; now I resign myself to waiting at Nimpo until the pilots tell me that my lake is open.

And now I'm sprawling on a padded bench in the bay window that doubles as my bed at night, looking across a half-kilometre of grey, ruffled water scattered with islands. It is a dullish, rain-spitting day with a bit of wind. A dark belt of forested shore defines the far side of the lake, and beyond this, three low peaks still thickly plastered with spring snow rise above the treeline. Two of the peaks, equally rounded and apparently of the same size from this perspective (although the farther one is in fact much higher), sit side by side on the left, and the third, on the right, is joined to them by a sway-backed saddle.

During my first winter here, I was struck by the resemblance of the mountain's silhouette to the body profile (sans head) of a young woman portrayed by François Boucher in 1752. The girl—she is no more than a teenager—is pert, sexy and naked, and is lying on a couch, three-quarters facing the viewer. She was one of Louis XV's mistresses, reputedly an Irish lass called Louise O'Murphy. Poor soul—I wonder what kind of life she had when her looks no longer served her. Would she ever have imagined that her brief moment of social ecstasy would earn her a place in art history books? She would certainly never have guessed, and would have had little consolation in knowing, that her name now graces a harsh pile of wintry rocks in the Canadian wilderness.

Although a much more dramatic vista unfolds toward the head of the lake, I designed both the orientation of my dwelling and the location of the windows in it to do full justice to Louise O'Murphy as well. For it is she who hosts the sunrise. On the shortest day, the sun first appears to the extreme right of her shoulder hump. As the year progresses, the emergence point moves slowly east, and when it clears the mountain completely, it marks the equinox. In spring, when this milestone is reached, I can look forward to the season of light; in the fall it presages the struggle I must soon face to cope with the lengthening hours of darkness. I am a child of the sun. I need natural light as much as a starving man needs food. I once visited an elderly lady who lived in sheltered accommodation and had all the health and bodily care facilities she could wish for as long as she was able to pay $1,500 a week. (I guess they don't charge by the month in those places: you might not live that long.) Her room had a single

Louise O'Murphy

window, and it faced north. She would never again in her life feel the sun on her face or its warmth permeating her bones. For me, the only thing worse would be to have no window at all.

Louise O'Murphy has a second importance in my life because she is also my gateway to the outside world. I could reach the nearest road by going straight down the river for a while, then wade across it near the head of Banana Lake, climb the far side of the valley there and cross a low pass to get into Maydoe Creek. From there it is a straight run—albeit a very brushy one full of windfalls—down to Charlotte Lake.

This route misses Louise O'Murphy altogether and is in fact the quickest way out, but it is a mess of swamp and fallen trees with few interesting views. I still use it if the weather is bad and the snow

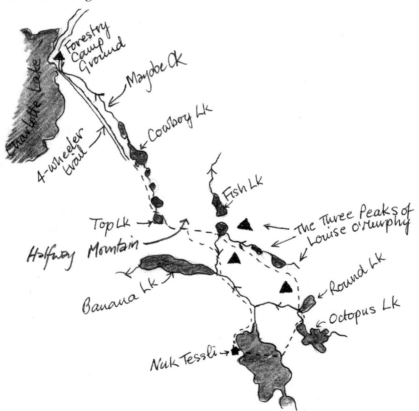

The route to the road.

is not too deep—one section is notorious for avalanches—but most of the time I prefer to head across my lake by canoe, climb the south boundary of my valley, then hike in a big curve on a well-marked trail I built myself, to Louise O'Murphy's shoulder. A high alpine valley runs behind it and continues right between her buttocks (as it were) before dropping slightly below the treeline to Fish Lake (so called, locally, as it is a frequent fly-in destination for people who want to go fishing for the day). The dip in the horizon that accommodates Fish Lake is where the sun rises during the equinoxes. Then follows another low peak, which I have dubbed Halfway Mountain because of its location on my trek, and on the far side of that, I can pick up the trail down Maydoe Creek.

Some people imagine that my ability to get around this wild country borders on the superhuman; that I must be "a six-foot, 200-lb. Amazon," as one kind gentleman wrote. (Actually, his figures were not too far out.) But in fact I am a slow walker and always have been. That may have been one of the reasons I soon lost interest in hiking with groups. I was always so exhausted trying to keep up, I could never enjoy what I was doing.

The distance to the nearest road on the map is paltry—maybe 30 kilometres—but the shortest time that it has ever been hiked is fourteen hours, and that happens only when the ground underfoot is dry and the creeks are not too tricky to cross easily. I used to make the journey in a single day when the conditions were good, but now I always plan to camp out for at least one night, usually on one side or the other of Halfway Mountain.

There are two other windows in my cabin at Spinster Lake. The one to the left of the bay window, the kitchen window, is small. Designed to allow light onto the countertop, it faces northeast and frames the sunrise on the longest day. It is through here that I see the northern lights in winter and the tail of the Great Bear as it hangs vertically in the small hours of an October night, indicating that dawn is not far away. Farther left, right under the pole star itself, is the highest point of a long alpine slab of land that divides my branch of Whitton Creek

from the next one. I call it the North Ridge and it is the most easily accessible alpine area from my cabins. Various small bumps along the ridge (including the aptly named Mammaries) give spectacular views, and below them a large, spring-fed flattish area is host to calendar-picture displays of alpine flowers: red paintbrush, blue lupine, white valerian, purple fleabanes and two species of yellow daisies.

The most dramatic view from the cabin looks toward the head of Spinster Lake. It is dominated by two peaks that are both much larger than any in the Charlotte Alplands. These are high enough to harbour extensive glaciers, and they retain many smaller snowfields year-round. Mount Monarch, on the left, rises to 3,700 metres. It is the tallest in the Tweedsmuir Provincial Park. To the right is Migma Mountain, a little over 3,000 metres. (I am reliably informed that if a mountain is named after a thing, the topographical designation should come after the name, i.e. Monarch Mountain. But if it is named after a person, the designation should come *before* the name, i.e. Mount Migma. Now if that's not nitpicking I don't know what is. The names I have used are the ones I first heard and that is how they will always be known to me.) Hidden behind smaller land barriers, unless one climbs away from the shores of the lake, are hundreds of peaks, rivers and glaciers spreading north, south and west.

It looks as though one could simply hop in a canoe, paddle to the head of Spinster Lake and reach these icefields in a matter of hours. But there are two reasons why this is not possible. First, although Monarch's summit fills the senses when one looks in that direction, it is much farther away than it looks—about 35 kilometres all told. Second, there is between us a vast north–south trench, totally hidden from my cabin, which drops a thousand metres and has very few routes down its precipitous sides. At the bottom are lush, virgin coastal forests, wild rivers, horrendous swamps—altogether some of the roughest country I have ever tried to hike through. One of the very few game routes joining the Charlotte Alplands to The Trench runs over the low, treed pass directly between Monarch and my window; it was through this pass that I first came to Spinster Lake. There is no obvious route near the top where the topography is less steep; the country there is heavily brushed and the going is slow. Through the bluffs crowding together near the bottom of The Trench, however, winds a track so well used that where there are patches of duff between the rocks it has been carved ankle-deep by the passage of paw and hoof. Along the rocky stretches, some parts are so precipitous I had to take the packs off my dogs so they could get up them. But droppings and footprints of deer, wolves, bear and even moose showed that these animals use the route like a freeway.

At the bottom of the bluffs is a swamp of Brobdingnagian proportions. Car-sized humps and corresponding hollows full of water are laced with 5-metre willows whose trunks lie as much horizontal as vertical and are a nightmare to fight through. It is another place where the dog packs have to be loaded onto humans, this time to keep their contents dry.

This swamp, which is about 8 kilometres long, is a watershed for the two river systems that occupy The Trench. South-running waters accumulate in Knot Lake before entering the Klinaklini drainage, whence they exit the continent through Knight Inlet. Knot Lake is a long stretch of water well supplied by the runoff from Monarch's icefields, and is consequently full of glacial flour. This fine, suspended silt reflects the light, and from a distance the lake is a wonderful turquoise green. But to get there from the swamp necessitates finding a route across Pandemonium Creek. The creek must have been dammed by a rockslide during heavy fall rains fifty years ago, then blown out when the pressure of water became too

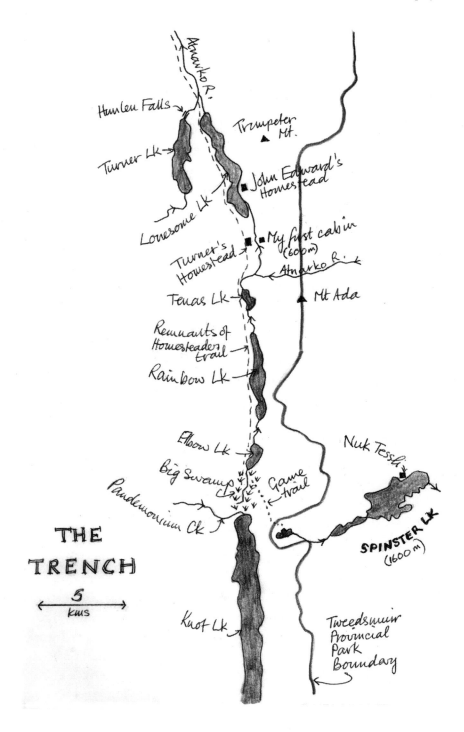

THE
TRENCH

5
kms

great. Huge cutbanks line the creekbed, and water and debris were spewed across the valley with such force, mature firs and cedars were sliced off at the base. New islands of boulders were created and they split the creek into many branches, all of which rage year-round because they are glacier-fed. Crossing them is an exercise of faith, as it is impossible to see the bottom through the suspended silt. One puts one's foot into the swirling icy water and hopes that it will soon touch something solid. Where banks of silt were formed above the water level, a new forest has sprung up, but these trees are as thick as palings on a fence. The only way I could get through them was to crawl on hands and knees, shoving my pack in front of my face. The Trench, then, is no place for the Sunday stroller.

North of this terrible swamp, a trail was once built, although it would take a pretty experienced bushman to find it now. It was created by the homesteaders who pre-empted property around the head of Lonesome Lake, 15 kilometres north along the Atnarko River. The original pioneer was Ralph Edwards, made famous by Leland Stowe's book *Crusoe of Lonesome Lake*. Ralph had three children: the two boys went out to make their way in the world, but the youngest, Trudy, moved 4 kilometres south and staked her own claim when she was still a teenager. She met Jack Turner and got married, and they had a daughter, Susan. Sometime after their homestead was established, the boundaries of the Tweedsmuir Provincial Park were extended to enclose the part of the Atnarko that lay in The Trench—it is a major salmon-spawning stream—and the eastern park boundary now follows the forested horizon I see from my window.

My first foray into the wilderness was down at the Turners' homestead. I had gotten to know Trudy and Jack through mutual friends, and was very taken with the idea of living close to nature as they did. Such an existence seemed exciting and romantic, but I did not feel that the doing of it was in any way extraordinary. I was, however, amazed when the Turners offered to let me build on their property. This was a dream come true. I had never built a cabin before, nor used a chainsaw, but I was no stranger to carpentering.

My father made custom furniture and restored antiques for a living. I grew up playing with woodworking tools and, more importantly, the idea that if I wanted anything, I could make it. By the time I arrived at Lonesome Lake, I had also spent hundreds of hours in mountain ranges around the world, and had long ago learned to love solitude.

The Turners hauled my logs with their horses and showed me simple methods of raising them with levers and pulleys, but I did all the falling and construction work myself. I learned to use a chainsaw, notch logs and cope with life 30 kilometres from the nearest road, and over 100 kilometres from the nearest store.

So when I left there four years later and came to Spinster Lake, I had a number of skills that were to stand me in good stead. I would have no horses or other human beings to help me lift things, but the trees up here were smaller. I had a block and tackle, a come-along and a peavey, and figured I could move anything I wanted to.

Not long after I left Lonesome Lake, Jack and Trudy sold their property to the Tweedsmuir Provincial Park and moved down the Atnarko into the Bella Coola Valley. Stanley, Trudy's eldest sibling, lived for a while some distance north of Lonesome Lake (but still several kilometres from the road); he died there just before Christmas in the year 2000. The only human resident at Lonesome Lake at present is the middle sibling, John, now in his late seventies. His lifelong dream has been to restore the homestead that his father built. It was left empty for many years while John worked outside, but he is happily ensconced down there, painting and carpentering, studying nature, and encouraging the deer, martens and foxes to feed from his hands. John is my closest neighbour and the only one in that direction for some considerable way. The overall distance between us is not great—a matter of some 25 kilometres—but because of the roughness of the country, it would take me three days to reach him on foot. By float plane, the journey could be completed in minutes.

CHAPTER 2

Wwoof! Wwoof!

Dear Nick,

You will remember, last fall, that I started to build a trail to Wilderness Lake. I figured I could incorporate the new cabin that was flown up there into a hiking tour and I want to get the trail established as soon as possible. I've more or less fixed the route and done some of the brushing out—it's going to be a very pretty trip as part of it goes along the river and part by several shallow lakes that reflect the mountains in several different directions. It used to be a terrible bush-bash up there but the hike should take only four or five hours when the trail is done. When the next lot of wwoofers come, I'm going to take them up there so that we can finish the job.

—Letter to Nick Berwian, July 10, 2001

I worked completely alone for several years when I first came to Nuk Tessli, but friends knew of some young Germans who were footloose for several months in Canada and who would welcome a period of time in the wilderness. One of these was "German Nick" Berwian, who did a lot of the grunt work and the bulk of the heavy carpentering for Cabin Three. On Nick's first visit, he was accompanied by his girlfriend Ellen, and it was she who told me about "wwoofing."

The repeat of the *w* in the word is no accident. The acronym stands for Willing Workers On Organic Farms. "You should contact them," said Ellen. "This would be a fantastic wwoofing place."

Nuk Tessli was not exactly an organic farm, but I wrote to the wwoof organizers and was welcomed as a host. I paid 35 dollars for a 25-word listing in the Canadian wwoofer book, and prospective wwoofers paid 45 dollars to access the information. It was the simplest, most straightforward arrangement that one could wish for. Wwoofers come from all over the world; they are required to work for board and lodging only. Hosts are expected to treat them more as family than as hired labour, and to ask for no more than four or five hours' work a day.

My first wwoofer applicant was a young man from Ontario by the name of Scott Williams. Only seventeen years of age, he had done quite a lot of canoeing and camping in Ontario, often alone, but he had never been west before and consequently had never seen a mountain. I explained to him that the work would require a lot of physical energy and would consist principally of hauling firewood by canoe and brushing out trails. I warned Scott that it was impossible to give him a four-hour day as it sometimes took that long to commute to the work site and back: would he be happy with working full days and then taking the same number of days off?

The next requirement was to organize his method of getting to Nuk Tessli. Even reaching the float-plane base was a problem for someone without a car, for there is no public transport along Highway 20. Nimpo Lake was four hours west of Williams Lake or two and a half hours east of Bella Coola—from either place, the only way for a person without a vehicle to travel was to either charter an aircraft or hitchhike.

Once Scott reached Nimpo Lake, there was still the difficulty of getting him into the mountains. If there had been a suitable client's flight with space on board, I could have squeezed him in and shared the cost, but 2001 was a sparse year for tourists and no one was coming during July when Scott was going to be in British Columbia. Paying a full charter fee for a plane was not an option for either of us.

The only other solution was for him to come in on foot. With his lack of experience, he obviously could not travel on his own.

Neither did I want to hike all the way out to Nimpo to fetch him—it would take four days out of my summer. But I didn't mind going halfway, especially as a friend, Naomi Dunaway, who had helped me for a month the year before, wanted to come back again. She had hiked in with me on one occasion and hiked out on another, plus she had completed a solo overnight trip in an area where there were no trails at all. I figured that if she and Scott got together, they could use my truck (which had been left at the float-plane base) to drive along the logging roads to the trailhead. Then all they had to do was follow Maydoe Creek to its source (see map, p. 25).

The first few kilometres from Charlotte Lake, originally a horse trail, had now been cut out for four-wheelers by pine-mushroom pickers so would be easy to follow. However, once Cowboy Lake was reached, the trail would become less easy to find. When I first came to Nuk Tessli, I hiked out for mail every month and spent hundreds of hours en route, linking bits of trap and animal trails, creating new sections and brushing the whole thing out. But now my correspondence comes on clients' planes so I rarely use the trail and have not bothered to maintain it. It has become just as overgrown and difficult to sort out as when I first put it together.

Near the head of Cowboy Lake is a dreadful bog that flows right to the edge of the lake. I had spent hours trying to find a way around it, taking routes farther and farther away from the shore, but without success. I warned the hikers that if they had not lost the trail before the bog, they would surely lose it then, but not to worry: all they had to do was follow the water, either lakeshore or river. The bush-bashing would slow them down a bit, but they would soon pick up the trail again. In any case, the trail itself was so bad they would hardly make better time if they were on it. The valley was narrow, there were no other confusing watercourses, and they could not possibly get lost.

Top Lake, on the Nimpo side of Halfway Mountain, was where my blazes ended and the trackless alpine stretch began. With a map and enough experience, the route was easy enough to follow—after all, I had found my way along it the first time—but the alpine could be confusing if visibility was poor, and the uppermost part of the trail I had built at the west end of Louise O'Murphy was difficult to find. So I proposed to meet Scott and Naomi at Top Lake. They could not miss the rendezvous, because the stunted, 150-year-old trees that used to grace the north side of the outlet had been flattened and dragged from their root holes by a huge avalanche a few years before. Naomi would remember camping there when she had hiked there with me last year.

I had a longer trek than they did, so if we set off on the same day they would likely arrive first. However, I warned them that they were not to attempt the alpine section without me under any circumstances. Should the weather turn poor, we would go down to Banana Lake and up the river to Nuk Tessli, and people really had to know what they were doing to attempt that route. I would leave a map and detailed written instructions at the cabin I used at Nimpo Lake, and when they arrived there, the two wwoofers should go to the owner, Mary Kirner, and Mary could call me by radiophone if they had any questions.

Scott and Naomi hitchhiked from Williams Lake to Nimpo during what amounted to the first real rain of the summer. The grey weather had not lasted long after I flew home, and the previous two weeks had been gorgeous. But as the clouds slowly parted to reveal Louise O'Murphy's flanks on the morning of the proposed hike, fresh snow could be seen well below the treeline. It was July 15, which is St. Swithin's day—whatever weather occurs then is supposed to last another forty days and forty nights. I told Naomi on the radiophone that she had better wait another 24 hours in the hope of some improvement. She should come to the radiophone again at 8:00 a.m. the following morning and we would make a decision then.

The 16th was pretty unsettled-looking at Spinster Lake, with columns of fog clinging to the land masses, but it looked better toward Nimpo, and Naomi said the sun was shining at her end. So we agreed to set off.

I had been very busy building a woodshed and doing some trail work closer to the cabin so had not been above the treeline for several weeks. I put the two dogs I had then, Max and Ginger, and our three packs into the largest canoe and paddled across my lake. I climbed the ridge on the south side and began the long slog up Louise O'Murphy's shoulder. The dry, cold spring had produced a poor showing of flowers around home so I was pleasantly surprised, once the forest began to thin out, to see all manner of species beginning to open up. The heathers were spectacular—white, rosy and yellow. In places, the white ones were so thickly blossomed it was like walking on snow.

The lupines were making a good show, too, although they would need another week to be at their best. Baby birds were everywhere—grouse, ptarmigan, pipits, savannah sparrows, golden-crowned sparrows and juncos. On the north-facing shoulder of Halfway Mountain, where there were still a number of snow patches, I surprised a cow cariboo with a very young calf.

The weather was not too bad on my side of Halfway Mountain,

Heather

but the wind was from the north, and early in the summer that circumstance almost always produces thundery weather. Soon, towering clouds built up, very dark below and blinding white above, dragging intermittent curtains of rain and hail over mountains that were patchworked with shadows. Fortunately, most of the precipitation missed me. Around Halfway Mountain, however, it was a different story. Lowering over Maydoe Creek was a solid black mass of vapour. Somewhere under that lot were Naomi and Scott. Exactly where was anyone's guess, for there was no one at the campsite to meet me.

This was surprising, because even if they had lost the trail, the hikers should not have taken more than six hours to get there after they had parked the truck. But perhaps they had become confused on the logging roads, which change every year as new cutblocks are created. Or maybe something had happened to my truck: it was old and unreliable, and if they had been forced to walk the logging roads, that would set them back a day.

It rained on and off during the night but the sun rose into a clear sky and the weather took a turn for the better. I made a comfortable chair for myself from my sleeping mat, backpack frame and a couple of poles wrenched from the trees that had been knocked down by the avalanche. I lit a smudge to keep away the bugs and prepared to enjoy my morning. I assumed the two hikers would arrive very soon, all apologetic for the delay, but the birds sang, the creek chattered, the bugs whined and nothing else disturbed the serenity of the landscape.

From my comfortable seat I looked directly across the little valley to the north face of Halfway Mountain. A snow-fed creek tumbles down the middle of it, and when the sun hovers over this, I've always figured it must be close to noon. Still no sign of the hikers. Had they smashed into a logging truck along the road? Met the grizzly that hangs around the Forestry campground every summer? Been shot by a serial killer? (I had brought a murder mystery along with me: not the best reading material when you are waiting for someone who is overdue.) I had my lunch and hiked down to the foot of the next lake, where I also often camp and maintain a firepit; perhaps Naomi's memory had failed her and she saw the ashes and thought that was to be our meeting point. But there was no sign that they or anyone else had been there this year. The patches of mud and sand in the trail were as devoid of footprints as a freshly raked Zen garden. I stamped my boots deeply into these surfaces: if the hikers did make it that far, they would know that I was not too far away.

Back at camp, I resolved to wait one more night. If they didn't turn up, I would have to get to a phone. Because I knew the way, I could reach the Forestry campground at Charlotte Lake in four hours, but if I did not meet the hikers, there would be no vehicle waiting for me and I would have to travel over 30 kilometres of logging roads before arriving at Highway 20 and a phone. Someone might be using the campground, or a logger might be driving on the roads, but at this

Top Lake camp

time of year neither was likely. It might very well take me two days to reach a means of communication if I went that way.

Going back home, however, would take ten hours at the most, so although I was heading away from the road, that seemed the most logical route to take. I set off at first light and must have arrived at Nuk Tessli around the middle of the afternoon.

I called Mary at once and asked her what had happened to my hikers. "I haven't the faintest idea," she replied. "They took your truck and left right after you spoke to them three days ago and I haven't heard a thing from them since."

I speak with Mary via a private local frequency that the owners have kindly let me use. My radiophone rarely works long distance but if I can't get through on the Telus channel, I often ask Mary to relay messages for me. So it was she who called the RCMP, and she eventually told me a corporal was on his way to her resort to talk to me directly.

I left the phone switched on and began to unpack my wet camping equipment. Mary's voice came back through the speaker. "Are you there, Chris?"

I walked over to the phone and depressed the transmit button. "Go ahead, Mary."

"You'll never guess what," she said. "Scott and Naomi just walked in the door!"

They had found their way to the Forestry campground along the logging roads without a problem, and easily picked up the four-wheeler trail to Cowboy Lake. They knew it was Cowboy Lake because they ran into a couple of people on bikes employed by the sawmill at Anahim Lake, who were flagging a route for a proposed logging road up there. In all my tramping back and forth, I have met other users of this trail only three times: for Scott and Naomi to encounter anyone was extremely unusual. They would have been little more than three hours from my footprints at that point, but instead of following the river up the valley, they spent the next two days simply going around in circles. They said they had kept finding blazes but they simply petered out. Judging by their description, they must have reached a point that was less than half an hour below the mud puddles I had stamped in. They even saw a rocky knob that I had told them was a good landmark, as it could be seen from many points along the valley, but for some reason they neglected to use it as a reference point. Then they started running into lichen-covered rocks that they thought they had seen before, and "mysterious footprints" that were probably their own—or maybe even mine, but I don't think they went that high up the creek. They were soaked from the rain, which had been a lot heavier on their side of Halfway Mountain, and bitten to death by the bugs. Scott told me later that he would have simply followed the water, but he was a very quiet and polite fellow and still young enough to accept that Naomi, who was older and had more experience in this type of environment, would know what she was doing. Eventually they gave up and managed to find their way back to the truck.

Sometimes a float-plane company will give me a cheaper flight if they are heading in the same direction as Spinster Lake, so I suggested over the radiophone that Scott and Naomi phone around and see what they could come up with. With luck, Gideon Schultz of Sharpwings (who was by then installed at the old Avnorth dock) was heading my way and he was able to drop the hikers off.

I put the wwoofers to work at once. The St. Swithin's day rule was holding sway, and the weather continued to be damp and rainy, although precipitation was never very heavy. Despite this, Scott and Naomi accomplished an enormous amount of work during their short stay.

Their first job was firewood. I chainsawed for a few hours in the rain, and they dragged the log rounds to the shoreline, loaded them into the canoes, paddled them home, then carried them in their arms to the woodshed.

This is a very labour-intensive job, and it takes me a good three weeks to accumulate enough for the winter when working alone. Next we built a bridge across the river where it runs out of my lake. I had spanned a couple of other creeks with fallen logs at different times, but this was the widest and wildest stretch of water I had

Canoeing the wood home

yet tackled. At this time of year it was still fairly full with spring runoff and impossible to wade. One tree was situated absolutely perfectly and I managed to fall it exactly where I wanted it. But one-log bridges are always a bit scary, particularly without a handrail, and I wanted to put another log beside it and eventually flatten both of them by cross-hatching the tops with a chainsaw and axing off the surplus. The chainsaw work would have to wait until the river went down—it was a one-person job in any case—but the wwoofers would be a lot of help in moving the second log. I was able to drop another tree across the water a few metres upstream. We lopped off the branches and inched the log to and fro with the come-along and peavey, which necessitated hopping back and forth over the river on the log already in place. The second log was thinner, not as straight and much more bouncy than the first, and when the water lost some of its power, I would have to build a support underneath as well as tie the two logs together with cross poles at either end. But I could easily do all that alone: to all intents and purposes, the river was now well and truly bridged.

The next task I wanted the wwoofers to help me with was the trail to Wilderness Lake. The cabin that had been flown up there was owned by Mary, and it was situated in spectacular hiking country. There were a number of stretches along the trail that still needed brushing out, but I decided that Naomi and Scott would

Mary's cabin

be better employed in hauling rocks. I wanted to erect a series of cairns as markers across the upper alpine stretch. In order to give the wwoofers some time off, I suggested that they work on the way up, then stay up there for an extra night and go for a hike: their goal, weather permitting, was to climb Wilderness Mountain.

The hike up to Wilderness Lake went as planned. On our way up I scouted ahead, tying flagging tape to twigs and stones where I

Building cairns

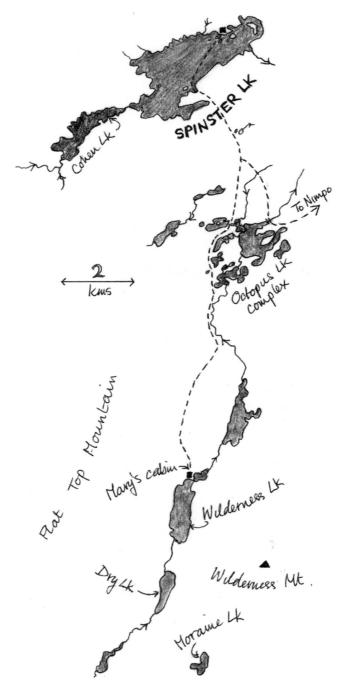

Cohen Lk

SPINSTER LK

To Nimpo

Octopus Lk Complex

2
kms

Flat Top Mountain

Mary's cabin

Wilderness Lk

Dry Lk

Wilderness Mt.

Moraine Lk

Wilderness Lake

thought the cairns should go, and Scott and Naomi packed rocks. After a while they became really creative and built some wonderful structures. A few of these fell over fairly quickly—this happens everywhere; I rebuild dozens of cairns every year—but others have remained just as they constructed them.

The following morning, Naomi and Scott set off on their expedition. The weather did not look all that promising and I gave them the necessary warnings about weather and other dire events. I worked alone for about three more hours on the trail before picking up my share of the camp and heading home. Despite the poor weather, Scott and Naomi climbed the mountain and found their way back to my place without difficulty. The partially constructed trail was still a bit confusing in places, so they had done well and I assumed their problem with the hike in from the road had simply been an aberration.

Soon it was time for the wwoofers to leave. I had planned on taking them to Top Lake again—surely they could not possibly go wrong going down Maydoe Creek this time—but was having some problems with my knee, which I had twisted on my dash to the phone. If I guided them, we would have to travel at half the speed and would need to leave a day early.

But both wwoofers were now confident they could find their way out. I replaced their map (the first one had disintegrated in the rain while they were thrashing around in circles) and took them to the wharf so I could point out the route to them on Louise O'Murphy and Halfway Mountain. "If the cloud is socked in up there," I told them, "you are on no account to try and cross Halfway Mountain, as you could easily miss the pass into Maydoe Creek. As long as you can see where you are going, you should be okay." Without me to slow them down, they were sure they would be able to reach the Forestry campground in a day. Even if no one was there and they could not hitch a ride, they reckoned they would still reach Highway 20 by the end of day two; with that in mind they elected to pack only one night's food.

I took them across the lake in the canoe, and off they went. Over the next couple of days, I periodically checked Halfway Mountain, but although the sky was sporadically cloudy, the mountains remained clear: visibility would not be a problem for them. I called Mary on the evening of the second day, but the hikers had not turned up. I assumed they had been unable to get a ride on the logging roads and were taking a little longer than they thought. But when they had not contacted Mary by the third evening, my heart sank. Surely they could not be doing this to me again!

I had impressed upon them that if either of them had an accident, they must stay together and light a fire—someone would fly over and spot the smoke and that would be the safest and surest way to be rescued. But by now, the weather had deteriorated into drizzle and rain, and visibility had become too poor for anyone to get up in an aircraft. Moreover, it was, inevitably, Friday afternoon. The nearest RCMP detachment at Anahim Lake, 20 kilometres from Nimpo, boasted four officers. But they shut down for the weekend, and all calls are diverted to Kamloops, an eight-hour drive away.

Mary called the Anahim Lake detachment on the land phone and, with the radiophone in one hand and the land phone in the other, relayed the conversation back and forth between the corporal and myself. The first thing he wanted to know was the missing persons' names. The second was: "What are they wearing?" I suppose it is the standard question for a missing persons form, but it seemed rather ridiculous under the circumstances. From what I remembered, their clothes were drab and nondescript, but it wouldn't have mattered. If any hikers at all had been seen anywhere between my place and Nimpo Lake, they could only be Naomi and Scott.

RCMP policy is not to look for missing persons until 24 hours have elapsed after their disappearance, but I convinced the officer that the 24-hour deadline was all but over, and if he thought that was a bit of a grey area, the hikers were definitely more than 24 hours overdue at the Forestry campground at Charlotte Lake. Given the double situation of the deteriorating weather and the upcoming weekend, I suggested someone should drive to Charlotte Lake and at least see if they could find any sign of them there. In the meantime,

I would pack for a two-day hike. If they still hadn't turned up by morning and the weather was good, I would wait for a plane and show the pilot and the corporal where the hikers had gone. If it was still socked in, I would start hiking over their route and try to find them that way. The only other people who would have a clue as to where to look on the ground would be the guide-trappers, and where they were at this time was anyone's guess. Nobody else knew anything at all about travel over the ground in the Charlotte Alplands.

A pilot who had been hearing our conversation over the radiophone volunteered to drive the RCMP officer to the Forestry campground. A short while later, his wife called me. "Did you hear that, Chris?" But the signal must have been deflected by a land mass: I had heard nothing. The pilot had apparently phoned his wife from his truck. He and the RCMP officer had driven partway along the road to Charlotte Lake—and had come across Scott and Naomi walking out to meet them.

Later, Naomi told me that this time she had become confused in the alpine. Although they could see for 20 kilometres in every direction, and they had the sun for a guide, they had struck off at right angles to the route they were supposed to follow. Fortunately, when it became increasingly obvious that they were far off course, they did eventually work out where they were and were able to reach Charlotte Lake. But by that time they were well into their second day. They were pretty tired and hungry when they finally got out to Nimpo.

CHAPTER 3

September 12

There has been a bear around for a few days. The first sign was fresh droppings on a trail near the cabin and then I saw the animal himself as he swam to one of the islands. I had just finished enclosing the porch, and as I stepped into it, the bear was perfectly framed by the new doorway. He was a fine-looking black bear, a boar judging by his size. He got out onto Big Island and puttered around on the rocks for a while, then burrowed into the trees and soon reappeared in the water on the far side. Fortunately the dogs were unaware of him and the bear was not at all concerned, merely doing his own thing in his own time. The lake was choppy—just enough wind was blowing to make whitecaps—but the bear was obviously very at home in the water. He looked around frequently and idly changed direction once or twice. When he was about three-quarters of the way across, he veered toward the mountains and paralleled the shore for some time before deciding to head to land. He gave himself a monstrous shake—what a lot of water those animals accumulate in their fur while swimming. Calmly, the bear ambled through the alder brush and disappeared.

—Journal, September 12, 2001

Some 60 kilometres north of Nuk Tessli, a unique valley hangs partway between the high Chilcotin Plateau and The Trench. It is about 8 kilometres long and is rimmed on the northern edge by a cliff of "organ pipe" basalt, which has given the valley its name, The Precipice. There are five properties in it. One is ranched full time but the owner no longer lives there, and in 2001 there were only two permanent residents, Dave and Rosemary Neads. Dave makes a living as a consultant on environmental matters, and in his various capacities must frequently attend province-wide meetings to talk to government and other users of the environment. This is quite extraordinary when you consider that the only access to this property is an abominable bush track along which it takes one and a half hours to travel the 30 kilometres between the Neadses' home and Highway 20, after which one must drive a further four hours to reach Williams Lake. In winter, an hour's battering on a snowmobile is often necessary to reach the public roads.

The Precipice is 60 kilometres from Nuk Tessli and it is the first inhabited land in that direction. A raven would take a bearing off the pole star to get there from my place, but it would be extremely difficult to travel that way on foot; the most practical way to do that is to go down into The Trench, follow the Atnarko River north for a while (bypassing John Edwards at the Lonesome Lake homestead by several kilometres), then pick up an old horse trail back up to the Neadses' valley. That journey goes through a lot of very rough country and would take at least four days. The quickest route in time is actually the longest in distance: to go to Highway 20 at Nimpo Lake, turn west to Anahim Lake and drive the logging roads down.

By a quirk of fate, The Precipice has a land phone. The telegraph line used to run through there long before there was any road to Bella Coola. During the last war, it was upgraded to voice, and because someone has always paid the bills, the phone has never been cut off. The connection used to be serviced by a line strung on rough little poles—it was the last party line to operate in western Canada—but recently a microwave tower was helicoptered onto the top of the basalt cliff.

Dave does a great deal of his consulting work by phone and email; finding the phone line too slow, he invested in a satellite connection powered, like all the Neadses' considerable array of electrical conveniences, by a large battery of solar panels backed up with a gas generator for long gloomy spells.

Because of the similarity of our lives, it is inevitable that we should be drawn together, and over the years we have developed a strong friendship. Staying in their house with a washing machine, dishwasher, running hot water, flush toilets, stereo, TV and coffee maker was luxury indeed, but the only thing I was really envious of was their internet connection. I knew The Nuk Tessli Alpine Experience needed a website, but a satellite hookup was far beyond my means and I couldn't see the point in having a website when no one could communicate with me by email. I could not imagine a web surfer fetching pen and paper, writing his request, then waiting six or eight weeks for a reply. When I grumbled to Rosemary about my predicament she said she would be happy to handle any email queries for me. She already did a great deal of computer work, some for her husband, some in relation to her stained-glass business and a lot for pleasure. Taking on my email business would be a pleasure for her, too, she maintained.

I bought a laptop so I could do my own email when I was travelling around on book tours, but we had to set up a communication system that would work when I was home. Rosemary could handle most of what cropped up, but she always liked to consult with me if possible. Dave and Rosemary were not a party to the local radiophone frequency so she could not phone me directly. I could sometimes get out on the long-distance frequency to her, but not very reliably. So we arranged that I would attempt to phone her on the weekend, when radiophone rates were cheaper. If I could not get through, Rosemary would fax her questions to Mary in time for my regular Monday afternoon call to her. If it was more urgent, Mary would call me. I did not have enough power to leave my radiophone on all the time, but arranged to tune in every day while I was eating supper, which was usually about an hour before sundown. Occasionally, as she had done with the RCMP officer at Anahim, Mary would have the land phone in one hand and the radiophone transmitter in the other and relay any messages back and forth.

A radiophone is anything but private, and I frequently heard other conversations. Since his brother Stanley had died alone in the bush at the end of the millennium year, John Edwards of Lonesome Lake has checked in twice a week with the owner of the radiophone frequency to let everyone know he is still alive and well. His timing is very accurate: Wednesday and Sunday, 6:00 p.m., without fail. I often lose track of the date, despite my efforts to keep a journal, but was always able to confirm what day it was by hearing John's voice. I knew, therefore, that the day the bear swam across the lake was a Wednesday, and a later look at the calendar showed me it was the 12th of September.

John usually described his interesting encounters with his martens, squirrels and pet fox, Vicky, but this evening's conversation was quite odd. It was apparent that John had been expecting an American visitor; the gist of the exchange was that as all commercial flying had been halted and the US border was closed, the American visitor was probably not going to make it. John and his counterpart at Nimpo Lake sounded quite casual, but I could make neither head nor tail of it. Why on earth would the border to the States be closed? Were we at war with the US?

I could have butted in and asked, but casual chat on the

radiophone is frowned upon, and I had no clue, from the calm way they were talking, as to the seriousness of the event. I would have to see if I could pick up a signal on the battery radio. These come through only during the dark hours, and then only if the atmospheric conditions co-operate. September days are fairly long, and it would be quite a while before the radio signal would be audible. It was a very peaceful, windless and golden evening. I read for a while and then, as the sun hovered on the rim of the world, switched on the radio. At first there was nothing but a faint hiss; then, as the sky darkened, an increase of static. Finally a few words faded in and out: I picked up "plane" and "crash."

As the last light left the sky, the signal suddenly strengthened. The incident was obviously one of great magnitude as none of the scheduled programs came on, only a continuous news broadcast. It still took me some time to understand what had happened because the trauma had occurred 36 hours previously and everyone was talking as if the whole world already knew about it. And I listened, stunned, in the soft, dark night, watching the stars emerge, while the story of the destruction of the World Trade Center unfolded. I went to sleep eventually and then put the radio on again and listened to it until the light came into the sky the following morning and the signal faded once more.

It was all so alien. The only pictures I had of the disaster were in my mind—I didn't even know what the World Trade Center looked like, although people kept referring to twin towers. I realized then why the last couple of days had been so exceptionally quiet. The sky had been totally empty of aircraft, both the high-altitude jets that I dimly hear now and then, and the local float planes that normally flew overhead three or four times a day at that time of year.

This, then, is how the world will end at Nuk Tessli. I won't find out about it until long after it has happened.

CHAPTER 4

The Winter of 2002

Minus 25°C and mist-snow. Snowflakes fine as dandruff fill the air with a texture not unlike the Scotch mist of the British highlands, except here the droplets are frozen. Mist-snows occur when cold fronts come down from the North; these air masses have a bitter bite to them far beyond what one would expect from the temperature recorded by the thermometer. In the more severe cases, eyelashes stick together and nasal passages freeze-dry with every breath.

—Journal, March 16, 2002

Woke to a diamond-clear sky full of stars. Thermometer recorded –33°C. Skied to the rim of Camp Meadow close to the alpine. The sun glorious, but the small wind too bitter to go away from the shelter of the trees.

A few creamy streaks of cloud behind Monarch, dulling the sun as it went down. Must still be warm down on the Coast.

—March 17, 2002

Warmed to –20°C and still quite a bit of mist-snow, but the sun shone through it when it rose this morning and created the most magnificent sundogs. There were three of them, one on top and one on each side of the sun. The flanking ones were the most vivid: brilliant rainbow slashes stabbing down in front of Louise O'Murphy and trailing out onto the ice. The upper one was paler, but the circle joining them was distinct and there was even a faint outer ring. It is the first time I have ever seen the second ring.

Streaky clouds behind Monarch at sundown again. If we don't get a dump of snow out of this I'll be amazed. Radiophone has been out for days. Even the local repeater fails when it ices up too much.

Cooked a pot roast and tried to make a Yorkshire pudding in a fry pan. Spectacular failure! (But I ate it anyway.)

—March 19, 2002

Over the years, Floyd Vaughn has been the pilot to transport me and my goods into the wilderness most frequently. Originally, he and his wife owned the only commercial air-charter company at Nimpo Lake, and I first met them when I wanted supplies delivered to Lonesome Lake. After I moved up to Nuk Tessli, the charter companies grew to three and the ownership chopped and changed, but Floyd flew for them as often as not, and he was always the only commercial pilot available in winter. Since Avnorth collapsed, there are no outfits operating commercially in winter at all.

Despite this, Floyd was still prepared to fly me home after the 2001 fall book tour; the only trouble was, he now no longer put skis on the Cessna 180, which had been the vehicle of choice before. Instead, he flew an Aeronca Champ, which was a great deal smaller and had a lot less power. There was room for only one passenger and very little extra space for freight. That was not too serious in itself, as Floyd would simply make more trips to haul my paraphernalia. The problem was the dogs—Ginger, a red husky mix, and Max, a 50-kilogram Akita cross malamute. Ginger had a lot of faults, but she loved vehicles and would be able to ride in the plane unaccompanied. Max, however, hated flying at least as much as I did. Ever since he had been a puppy he had loathed vehicles of any kind. If he had the slightest indication he was going to ride in a car or plane, I would never be able to catch him. I would have to tie him up long before he could hear the motor.

Floyd had flown Max a number of times and knew that if he was restrained, he would be okay. He had often helped me load the struggling dog, pushing first a nose, then a foot, then a tail inside the plane so we could close the door. I had tried giving Max tranquilizers, but they never made him sleepy until after he got back on the ground. No matter how much he struggled, however, Max never attempted to bite.

Nobody had yet landed on my lake that winter so no one knew what the surface of the ice would be like. Experience has shown that once the Nimpo ice is good, it is strong enough on my lake, too. But Spinster Lake might have the additional problem of overflow. There was generally two or three times the snowfall at home as there was at Nimpo. Heavy snow pushes the ice down, and water wells up through the cracks. Even in very cold temperatures this water may remain liquid. As soon as the snow cover is breached, the water instantly freezes to whatever it touches. If that happens to be a plane's skis, the aircraft is unable to reach takeoff speed until the pilot has laboriously chopped off every last scrap of ice. If the air temperature is above freezing, the sogginess of the upper snow and drag of the water will also prevent the plane from being able to lift into the air. Overflow, then, was a potential disaster.

Floyd was an old hand at this sort of thing, though. He would do a test run, a touch-down at flying speed, then look down at his tracks to see if he could risk a landing. Water in the tracks would indicate overflow. He thought it was better to take a load of freight first as it would be lighter. I wholeheartedly agreed with this—I hate flying and did not want to risk having to be in the air for twice as long without getting anywhere.

So Floyd loaded some boxes aboard and took off. The round trip would take him an hour. I had driven my truck onto the ice in front of Mary's house and waited inside among her jungle of geraniums until Floyd's plane came swooping back.

Floyd said there was quite a bit of snow on the lake but the overflow was not too bad on the open part. He had landed there, then taxied to within the circle of rocks and islets that surrounds the cabins, but the overflow was worse close to shore, as it often is, so he had scooted back out to the open part of lake. Fortunately it was a mild day and the water he had plowed through did not freeze onto his skis. Carrying the boxes two at a time, he had slogged through calf-deep snow, breaking through into the water at times, and deposited the freight on one of the islands.

It was going to be much more difficult to "persuade" Max to get into the Champ than into the 180. Not only was the space much smaller, but also the plane had a fabric skin that could easily be damaged by a flailing dog's claws. I had brought along extra socks and twine with the idea that I would try to muffle Max's feet, but Floyd thought we could get away without doing that. The interior of the cockpit was lined with plywood; once inside, Max could not do any damage.

I had to climb in first, otherwise I would never have been able to get my seat belt on. The passenger accommodation was so low and restricted that from the knees down, my legs were spread on either side of the pilot's seat. Somehow we had to squeeze Max's bum into the tiny space between my lap and the back of Floyd's chair.

With me pulling, Floyd pushing and Max resisting and whimpering, we got him aboard and jammed his bum onto the floor. His heavy front paws, as big as a wolf's, were placed on my shoulders, and I linked my arms around his body to hold him. Flying is never

Inside Floyd's Champ

pleasant for me, but now I had to contend with a constant supply of hyperventilated doggy breath in my face as well.

On Spinster Lake, the plane's skis kept it out of the overflow, but as I stepped out, my sinking feet left footprints that were dark with water. Floyd had stayed beyond the ring of islands again and I would have the unpleasant task of tobogganing all my possessions several hundred metres through heavy patches of overflow to reach the cabin.

The snow level had been very low at Nimpo so I had brought no snowshoes with me in an effort to save space, which meant that it took an inordinately long time to slog through the wet stuff and struggle up to the cabin. My snowpacks were soon saturated, but just inside the door were another pair and dry socks. My numb feet would soon warm up when I got moving again. I lit the stove and put a metal pail of snow on top to melt. I grabbed the toboggan and snowshoes, which I had placed ready in the porch before I left, and slopped back to the pile of freight. I had time for only one trip before Floyd returned with his third load of the day. Already my snowshoe tracks were grey with sludge and I grumbled that it was going to take all day to get the stuff off the ice at this rate. "Well," said Floyd to cheer me up, "just thank your lucky stars you don't have to drag it all the way from Nimpo."

When I make prolonged trips outside, I am visited by intense flashes of longing for the sun and wind and peacefulness of home. The only thing that sustains me through the dark, dreary misery of December on the Coast is the knowledge that there will be an end to it and Nuk Tessli will be my reward. I imagine the euphoria of being in my own space and solitude, and count the days and hours until my return.

But once I am home, tranquility does not come all at once. The first days are often restless and disjointed. This feeling cannot be attributed solely to the tedious cleaning and organizing chores that have to be done. But soon I find myself taking pleasure in small remembered activities—the different foods I eat because of circumstance, the automatic movements to place things, the finding my familiar way in the dark. At that point, which takes place usually after a couple of days, I finally feel whole. The outside word drops away like the skin of an onion. The scratchy, brittle outer layer of my city-coping persona is peeled away and the moist inner core is exposed.

My preferred routine is to get up in the dark, as early as two or three in the morning. (I never use a watch, but when the radio signal is not baffled by snow or northern lights I generally listen to the news while eating breakfast, and someone mentions the time sooner or later. On clear nights the position of the moon and stars gives me a pretty good idea of how much darkness is left.) After a leisurely read, I tackle whatever writing project I have to hand: visual art work must wait for daylight, as the small electric light—or the candles I use if my batteries are low—are not adequate for painting or printmaking. The electrical system that runs the light and my old Mac Classic computer is powered by two small photovoltaic panels that convert the sun's energy into a usable form and feed it into deep-cycle storage batteries. These enable me to write for two days without sun. Although I sometimes have to husband the power if dull or snowy weather is prolonged, I can often manage four to six hours of electronic writing a day. If I need to conserve power, I scribble a longhand draft by candlelight in the dark hours, which means I can use the stored power more efficiently. By the time I have done all my brain is prepared to deal with, the sun is up and shining and I can get outside for a ski or chores like splitting wood and hauling water. In the winter of 2002 I was starting to put together *Snowshoes and Spotted Dick*, and reworking *Lonesome: Memoirs of a Wilderness Dog*. A publisher had expressed interest in this last manuscript, and I wanted to have it in the best state possible before I presented it to her.

I have designed the cabin so that when I work on the computer I can sit at an angle and see through either of the major windows. One afternoon while thus occupied, I noticed Max out on the ice near the island where the tree swallows nest, carrying what looked like an old, ratty sweater in his mouth. As a puppy he loved fuzzy things and would gleefully grab wool mitts and toques, then drop them in the deep snow where I could not easily reach them. Sometimes he grabbed a garment off the washing line, but this was winter and clothes were always brought inside to drip and dry. So what on earth was Max carrying? Through the binoculars I could see that his prize was a young otter—dead but still floppy so obviously very recently killed. No doubt Ginger was the murderer—she was perfectly safe with people but deadly with other animals. I went at once to investigate: the tracks came from the tree swallows' island but there had been no fresh otter tracks on the lake (and the deep, snowboard groove of otter tracks are unmistakable) so the animal must have been there without moving for some time. I had not heard any noise so there had obviously been no fight (and otters are very fierce creatures when cornered): no doubt the poor creature had already been close to death through sickness or starvation.

I thought I might as well get the carcass to feed the meat to the dogs and clean the skull for my large collection of nature objects. Max, however, decided he wasn't going to share. Still carrying the otter, he ran off the lake and up a trail that eventually went up onto the North Ridge. Past the outhouse, it was a ski trail only, and I kept

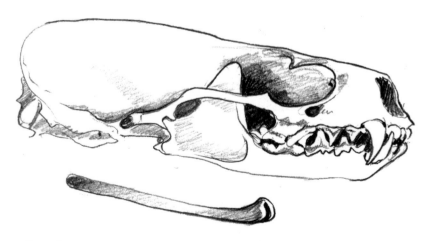

Otter bones

crashing through and had to go back to the cabin for snowshoes. I tied Ginger so there would be fewer complications, but by the time I arrived back at the point where I had to don the snowshoes, Max came running toward me, this time otter-free. I took him to the cabin and tied him up as well, then finally was able to go and look for the otter.

It was growing dark. There were two fresh deep furrows in the snow leading off the main ski trail, and each ended in blood-flecked snow. The otter was not visible in either, but the fresh tracks did not go anywhere else so it had to be there somewhere. I took off one of the snowshoes and dug around, and eventually found the otter jammed in a hole under a log. Max had managed to pile at least 30 centimetres of snow on top of it. The small animal was hardly bigger than a cat.

I planned to boil the carcass and feed it to the dogs in small amounts as treats. The best place to cut it up was on the ice. Watched avidly by the whining (and still chained) dogs, I pulled out the guts and discovered a very curious object. Right between the hind legs was a bone a bit shorter than my little finger. It did not seem to be attached to the skeleton, but was just floating free, encased in a tube of tissue. It could only be one thing: a penis bone.

Adrian Forsyth, in *The Natural History of Sex*, says that humans are among the very few animals that don't have these things. Their primary use is to help place the sperm as far along the female reproductive organ as possible, thus improving the chances of fertilization. A walrus's is 60 centimetres long, but small rodents like chipmunks and gophers also possess them.

Nature has designed the male animal not only to procreate but to also do the best he can to make sure his own particular genes are passed on—not conscious thought, of course, just one of the countless complicated idiosyncrasies that nature has evolved to encourage the constant competition a species needs to maintain to stay viable. Lions, for instance, will eat cubs of their own species to ensure that the female comes into heat and bears his own offspring. Adrian Forsyth describes some male rodents' attempts to exclude the genes of other males by sealing their sperm into a female's reproductive tubes with a waxy plug. The penis bone comes to the rescue once again as the animal's own, personal pry bar.

CHAPTER 5

Bucky

Dear Nick,

It looks like I'm going to be on TV again! Sometime in the New Year as far as I know. Dave Neads was approached by a team filming a series called Great Canadian Rivers *for local input. They are going to portray the Klinaklini. My lake actually runs into the Atnarko so my inclusion into the show is stretching things a bit, but most of the mountains you can see from the cabin are part of the Klinaklini watershed.*

—Letter to Nick Berwian, early September 2002
(I've lost track of the date again!)

The film people were going to do the bulk of their work by helicopter. However, they had scheduled a five-hour visit to my place, and at around 10:00 a.m. Tweedsmuir Air brought in a cameraman, a soundman, a producer, the cameraman's wife and a simply enormous mound of equipment. Most of it was in cases and unrecognizeable to me, but the video camera was huge. Apparently it cost $165,000 to buy, but the US company that sponsored the series had hired it for a mere $1,000 a day. The machine was at least as long as a man's arm and as wide as a slim torso. Just carrying it must have been a chore. The equipment also included some microphones encased in that hideous nylon fake fur that they use for the heads of kewpie dolls: apparently it cuts down wind interference. I warned them that Max was partial to fuzzy things, and sure enough they had barely turned around before the dog had one of them in his mouth.

Heavy tools and limited time meant that the film crew could not stray far from home. Fortunately it was a gorgeous day with a fresh breeze, sparkling blue lake and dazzling white mountains so there was a lot of good material close by. The cameraman took several shots of me paddling up the lake toward the mountains, and then he wanted to get in the canoe with me. I was using my latest canoe (obtained in a trade for a loom I was no longer using), because it was the only one whose gunwales were not trashed from hauling lumber and firewood. The problem was it was also the most tippy. I could not get my mind off the $165,000 camera at the other end of the wobbly boat as I was paddling along.

The filmmakers were not really interested in Nuk Tessli per se; they only wanted something they thought was entertaining and had a fixed picture of it in their minds. No doubt an eccentric old spinster living far from a road fitted their script quite nicely. Later on, we took a small walk. Max and I both wore backpacks. We were asked to hike in front of the camera; it was supposed to look casual so I was warned not to look at the lens. I had no trouble following instructions, but Max didn't know what to make of it. We started from the cameraman's left. At first, Max obediently followed, but then he stopped right in the middle of the shoot and stared directly at the cameraman. Back we went to the beginning. Started off fine— then, in the same place, Max did it again. After the third time, when he repeated his performance exactly, the producer guffawed. "He just wants to be a star," she said. We gave up after that.

Back at the cabin, they sat me on the deck and set up an interview. The producer asked me questions, but only my replies would be used on the show. The audience would not be aware of the monster camera, on a hefty tripod this time; or the soundman clutching his kewpie doll in one hand and fiddling with his large box of mechanical tricks with the other; or the producer with her clipboard; or the cameraman's wife holding a metre-wide disc of aluminum foil to reflect light into my partially shadowed face.

At one point I said, "This is bizarre. I have to get a picture of this." But their time ran out and things got packed up in a rush. Then the producer said, "Oh, you wanted a picture. We've just got time for a group shot." "It's not you I wanted," I replied. "It's all your stuff." At which the poor woman looked quite put out.

I'd had Ginger the red husky for nearly two years, but was finding one of her traits too difficult to deal with. She was wonderfully affectionate with all humans, enjoyed riding in vehicles and got on well with Max, but every time she met a female dog she tried to

Max on film

kill it. Alpha female sled dogs will do that sometimes. The breeder told me she had some wolf in her. The first altercations were merely scraps, but then she severely injured two different friends' dogs. During book-promotion tours I am frequently billetted in strangers' homes. When I am not lead-walking them, the dogs must live in the truck or be tied to it by chains. Dogs are a lot more aggressive when they are restricted like that, and our encounters with other canines in populated areas were getting too intense. So I found Ginger a home near Anahim, on a place that was some distance out of town, and during the 2002 spring book tour, I went to an animal shelter run by the SPCA. It happened to be in Burnaby, as the friends I was staying with took a particular interest in that branch.

Two criteria I insisted upon. One was that the dog had to be good with people; the other was that it must not be a barker. I absolutely cannot stand a yapping dog. A suitable size was also important, as was a good winter coat.

The Burnaby SPCA contained about sixty dogs, most of them housed three or four to a cage. The majority seemed to be black with tan legs, muzzles and eyebrows—in other words, Rottweiler crosses—and the rest showed traces of shepherd and pit bull in their makeup. All the breeds that some city dwellers consider cool, but that end up being too much of a handful for them. I later heard that the reason so many Rottweilers were incarcerated was because they are very good at looking fierce and barking their heads off when put on a chain; consequently, they are a favourite choice for marijuana growers. When the cops bust the grow-ops, the dogs get taken along to the SPCA.

I would have preferred a female and indeed took one for a couple of weeks, but she turned out to have a chronic back problem that induced lameness when she walked long distances. It was a pity, because she had a lovely disposition—she would still make someone a lovely house pet—but obviously she was not going to work for me.

On my initial visit, I had been struck by a powerful young Rottweiler-chow mix. He had not been cropped, that hideous practice that so many Rottweilers are subjected to, and he sported small flop ears and a vigorous bushy tail. He was the largest animal in the place, and the slightly squished chow nose gave him a very cute face. He was just in the process of being collected by a woman with children who was going to give him a trial run. But when I brought the other dog back, the Rottweiler was back in his cage, excitedly barking and leaping as all the other sixty canines were. Unfortunately it is extremely difficult to judge a dog's true character under these circumstances, but volunteer workers insisted he had the kind of disposition I needed, and I put him on a lead and introduced him to Max, who had been chained to the perimeter fence all the while. Although he had looked so big in the pens, the new dog was quite a bit smaller than Max. I expected a bit of snapping and snarling, and I was not disappointed. But when we let both dogs loose in a small enclosure, they seemed at least to tolerate each other, and I decided to give it a go. The new dog had not been neutered, so that had to be dealt with, and as I had slide shows to present up the Sunshine Coast but would be returning in a few days, my Burnaby friends volunteered to take the dog for that time and see to the surgery. When I picked him up again, he was wearing one of those plastic collars that look like buckets, so I called him Bucket–head for a while, soon to be shortened to Bucky.

When I reintroduced him to Max, there was a tremendous fight. Max was tied to the truck at that point and he might well have hated it, but he was certainly going to let this newcomer know it was his territory. However, once that battle was over, they showed very little animosity toward one another, though I was always very careful to make sure they could not reach each other's food. Nonetheless, I did not think it prudent to make them ride together right away in the dog crate at the back of my Suburban, but made a space for Bucky on the front seat. He loved vehicles and was easy to transport as long as I kept him restrained. Otherwise he wanted to jump all over everything in the vehicle's interior, including me. He made me hoot with laughter as he jammed the open end of his bucket collar hard against the windshield so he could see what was coming along the road. It must have looked very odd to oncoming drivers.

The book tour still had most of a month to run and neither Bucky nor Max was off the lead or chain in all that time. Being an early riser, I was usually up long before my hosts, and I always took the dogs out for an hour or so as soon as it was light enough to see. They had a shorter walk in the evening and another during the day if I could manage it.

Back at the Nimpo Lake Resort where I had my outside cabin, they still had to be restrained because Mary's hobby is small exotic birds and animals—she has ducks, geese, all kinds of funny breeds of chickens, guinea hens, peafowl, deer, llamas and a multicoloured tribe of tame rabbits. Most of these creatures run free, even though a number are periodically lost to owls, eagles, hawks and coyotes. If either of my dogs got among them, there would be carnage.

When I chained Bucky to Ginger's old kennel, under the next tree over from Max's, he barked non-stop and nearly drove me mad. So I dragged the kennel onto the sagging cabin porch. That shut him up all right—trouble was, I had allowed him too much chain and when my back was turned he pushed open the door (which could not be properly shut, as the frame was too warped) and managed to reach a pound of butter that was sitting on the counter. He wolfed the lot, foil wrapping and all. Fortunately I got him outside before he threw it all up again.

The Nimpo cabin was convenient and dirt cheap, and Mary has always been a very generous landlady, but I disliked the restrictions of having close neighbours and never stayed there any longer than I could help. A few days later, therefore, I loaded myself, dogs and some freight into Stewarts' 185 and returned once more to Nuk Tessli. I kept Bucky tied up for one more day so he would associate my cabin with dinner, then let him loose. I worried that he and Max might take to roaming and chasing game, and vowed that if they did they would have to take turns being tied up, but although they often took a morning hike into the meadow behind the cabins, they were never away very long.

Bucky still stole food, though. I have no fridge but keep things like eggs and butter and cheese on the floor near the door, where they stay pretty cool. I hate screen doors and take them off for the winter; as the biting insects do not usually come until the end of June, the door is often wide open during the early part of summer. It was the cheese that disappeared first. I could not understand where it had gone until I found the chewed, greasy wrapper under a tree. Bucky could dive into the cabin and gulp down his prize so quickly that if he had his eye on something I never had a chance even if I was standing right beside him. After a while he did accept that he was never allowed in the house (there were two insulated kennels in the enclosed porch) and when that happened, the "fridge" was sacrosanct again.

I made the mistake, when I first put a pack on my original dog, Lonesome, of giving her too much to carry. From then on she hated it. With subsequent dogs I have broken them in gradually. I give the dog a completely empty pack at first, just to get him used to the feel of something on his back. I bribe him with a treat and soon he learns to ignore the bag. On the next hike, the packs are stuffed out with something bulky, usually crumpled dog-food sacks: it is the width as much as the weight that the dog has to learn to cope with. I always use an old pack for this exercise: the dogs beat them up pretty severely on the rocks and trees as they barge into them. Some never learn to compensate for these obstacles. They are the dogs that go through a pack in a couple of seasons. I did not have packs small enough for Bucky but roughly adapted an old one of Ginger's. I would make one with a better fit before the end of June, as I planned to hike out to the road then—all the way this time—to meet some more wwoofers (of the two-legged variety).

Once the dog is used to the bulk, I start adding rocks for weight. For the month of June, every time we went anywhere, Bucky was slipped into his pack and given his cookie, and he now wore it with panache. When I was packing him in earnest, however, I would have to keep him on a lead because he liked to wade into every patch of water he could find, with the consequence that the packs became filled. The water ran out through the damage holes as soon as Bucky jumped onto dry land, but once he was packing in earnest, any contents of value would be ruined. While he was still wearing his training pack, however, he was allowed to run free.

The two dogs and I set off on an excursion two days before I was due to leave for Nimpo. Near the outlet of what local users call Octopus Lake (see map, p. 25), the trail crosses a two-log bridge.

Bucky

This was the first bridge I built, and because of the great scarcity of trees at this slightly higher altitude, it had taken me a couple of days working alone to get the logs into place. The trees were bumpy and uneven: I planned to flatten the top at some point but I had not yet managed to find time to do it when the water was low. To make the crossing easier for the time being, I wanted to string a rope from one side of the river to the other as a handrail. Part of the trail close by needed brushing out and I planned to make a day of it.

To familiarize Bucky with the land route around Spinster Lake, I did not cross the water directly but as I had done on more than one occasion already, canoed close to the shore and kept calling the dogs to encourage them to run alongside. Max was an old hand at this and knew the way well. Bucky wore his pack, the rope in one side and rocks in the other to balance the load. He was still using the beat-up saddlebags. Bucky loved to wade in water (though he steadfastly refused to swim, wearing packs or not), and by the time we reached Octopus Lake the rope and the dog-food bags were sodden.

The rocks came out of the bags when the rope did; after I had worked for several hours we returned home, Bucky now carrying an all but empty pack.

We were almost back at the canoe, slopping through a waterlogged meadow, when a moose leapt to its feet and galloped off. Away went both dogs in hot pursuit. I yelled like a maniac, but there was no stopping them. I waited for a while but was too wet and tired and hungry to hang about for long. Max always came back to me quickly if he became separated for some reason and, satisfied that Bucky also knew the way home, I left them to it and launched the canoe into what was by now a pretty windy lake. Half an hour after I got back to the cabin, Max flopped down on the deck. There was no sign of Bucky.

The wind was too strong for me to get back up the lake in a canoe. Walking round the edge and back would take a good two hours, and there was not enough daylight left to do it. The wind made shouting rather pointless, but I yelled a couple of times anyway. The dog was nowhere to be seen.

Bucky on the Octopus Lake bridge

The wind died during the night, and in the morning the lake was dead calm. I went down to the wharf when it was still dark and called for a while. At first light I started paddling around the lakeshore, retracing the route that Max would have taken, but there was no trace of the other dog. The outlet where Naomi and Scott had helped me build the bridge is directly across the lake from the cabin. It was roaring with spring runoff. On one occasion I had been swept off my feet while trying to cross it. Bucky had crossed the bridge a number of times and should have known his way. But because he liked being in the water, I wondered if he had gone into the river wearing his pack, and the bags had filled and carried him down. The river plunged through rocks and riffles for quite a way before spreading into a wide pool. Its edges were brushy with slide alder already dense with new leaves, and the body of a black dog might be difficult to spot among them, but his packs were red and would surely stand out well enough. I thrashed through the brush, checking every eddy, but there was no Bucky.

The meadow where the moose had been was one of a kilometre-long series that ended by the river. I slogged up through these swamps—knee-high water, tussocky sedge, short willows grabbing at my legs—and called and called and scanned the area with binoculars. I tried to follow the tracks where the moose had been, but there was too much water lying on the ground to sort them out. Max was no help—he was enjoying his hike but he never once looked alert as he would have done if either the moose or another animal of interest was close. In the end, my voice hoarse with yelling, I could do nothing but return home.

On the next two mornings, when it was calm, I canoed into the middle of the lake and called again. I was supposed to have started hiking to Nimpo by the second day of my search, but I went to the expense of hiring a plane just so I could leave 24 hours later. When Max and I were lifted into the air, Bucky had not returned. He had now been gone three days and I did not expect to see him again.

It was a week later before a Beaver, carrying Max, supplies, two wwoofers and myself, touched down again on my lake. As we taxied to the wharf I thought I saw a dark movement up by the cabin. No dog bounded to greet us, but as we unloaded the freight onto the wharf, something red began to slowly descend the little trail. To my utter amazement, there came Bucky, barely able to walk, with sunken eyes and dull, harsh coat, looking like a "before" picture in an SPCA cruelty-to-animals appeal. One of his front legs was jammed through the breast strap of his pack and this had gouged a big wound in his armpit.

At once I tied Max up to keep him out of the way. Getting the pack off Bucky was a bit of a chore because he snarled and tried to bite when I touched him. Then I gave him a handful of kibble. I did not want to feed him too much at once, as he would have eaten almost nothing for ten days. People have often commented that he must have been able to find wild food, but he was severely crippled by the pack's breast band, and even without the injury he would not have been able to run very fast. Bucky ate slowly, as if it were an effort, but it was amazing. At once, his eyes looked brighter! I fed him several times over the next couple of days and, apart from the wound in his armpit, which remained tender for a while, by the end of that time he had filled out, his coat was shiny and you would have never known there had been anything wrong with him.

I gave Bucky his new pack after that and resigned myself to keeping him on a lead whenever he was wearing it. I thought he might be pack-shy after his experience, but he still associated packing with cookies rather than pain, and the minute I picked one up, he came running over for his treat. He still ran free when he was unencumbered, but Bucky, it seemed, never learned. (Or perhaps it was me who had the learning problem: it took me quite a while to realize that I should never trust him.)

One day I went up onto the North Ridge with a client. It was the most gorgeous day—brilliant sun, blue sky and still lots of snow on the higher mountains. Although the south-facing slope of the North Ridge is usually free of snow at that time, wonderful cornices cling to the far side through most of the summer. Dogs love rolling in hard-packed snow, and Bucky at once ran out onto one of them. The snow, however, sloped down to the edge of the cornice, which hung several metres away from the cliff like a breaking wave. Below was a sheer drop of 20 or 30 metres. Bits of the cornice break off as the summer progresses and it is never possible to guess when that is going to happen. Wriggling on his back, Bucky began skidding toward the edge. I screamed my head off, but he ignored me completely. Finally he righted himself and calmly trotted back to me with a puzzled expression on his face. "What on earth are you making such a fuss for?" he seemed to say.

That was the first fright of the day. The highest point of the North Ridge is a peak we call Avalanche Lake Lookout. It affords spectacular views of the Coast Range, and it also hosts cliffs on both sides that are home to mountain goats. Max will chase these animals whenever he gets a chance (I try to anticipate this and restrain him, but I am not always successful at predicting where the goats will be seen). However, he is smart enough not to go over the cliff and I assumed that any dog would be put off by it. The last thing I saw of Bucky, though, was the tip of his bushy tail as he flipped over the top.

The client and I cautiously approached the edge and, by leaning precariously over it, could just see Bucky on a small ledge 20 metres below. There was no way I could climb down there, and it appeared that Bucky could not climb back up. I called for a while, but he just looked at me. Perhaps if I walked away, he would make more effort to come. Twenty minutes later he had not appeared and I trudged back up to the rim of the drop. Bucky was still in the same place. It was breezy and quite chilly on top, but the cliff blocked the wind and the sun shone full on him. He was beginning to look distressed from the heat.

Perhaps if I followed the edge of the cliff around for a while, calling the dog as I went, I could reach a lower point to which he might be able to scramble. The descent was not easy for me—the boulders underfoot were steep and loose—but all of a sudden Bucky decided he could do this and he effortlessly leapt across and came to me. I was pretty mad at him by this time. I did what I should have done sooner and put a string on him, keeping him by my side for the rest of the day.

Bucky has proved to be a chasing maniac. Moose, cars, grouse, squirrels, snowmobiles, horses, cows—if it moves, he runs after it, and if it doesn't, he keeps lunging at it until it takes off. All my dogs have chased running animals, but the others have usually given up after a short time. Bucky, however, is incorrigible. Was that story true, about all the Rottweilers in the Burnaby SPCA being rescued from grow-ops? Would he calm down if someone lit a roach and held it under his nose?

Bucky had one other annoying adventure (annoying for me—he enjoyed himself thoroughly) that summer when the *Great Canadian Rivers* film crew arrived. Five clients had been staying in one of the cabins; they had flown in the afternoon before and planned to spend three or four days hiking to another lake where they would be picked up by plane to return directly to Nimpo. They were just hoisting their packs onto their backs when the film crew landed, and in the confusion I never gave Bucky a thought.

It was perhaps half an hour later when I missed him. The clients had a puppy with them, and Bucky, who was still probably no more than two years old himself, had enjoyed great games with the pup the night before. When I realized he was no longer around, I thought he might have followed the hikers. At that point they were across the lake near the outlet. I could see them with the binoculars, but it was too brushy to see their own dog, let alone discern whether Bucky was with them.

The film crew was on a very tight schedule, and there was nothing I could do about a missing dog. After the crew had departed, I started the yelling routine again and continued to do it every calm morning and periodically throughout the next five days. The day the hikers had been due to fly back to Nimpo from the lake at which they had finished their trek, an unscheduled plane arrived at my dock. Sitting happily in it was Bucky. The hikers had not noticed that Bucky was following them until they had been walking for a couple of hours—too far, they felt, to warrant them returning. The clients would not let me pay for the extra flight, so at least Bucky's escapade had not cost me anything, but cute or not, I was pretty much ready to shoot the dog by that time.

People often comment, when they come to Nuk Tessli, on how quiet and placid my dogs are. This is because they are not shut up or chained most of the time. On the road it is a different story; then they are just as hyper as any city dog. People who know the animals only on book tours sometimes tell me I should train my dogs to be better citizens of society. But some animals are simply not very biddable: most sled breeds are a case in point. I can make them sit for their food, and come, and walk to heel—as long as there are no moose or cats to chase. Every dog I have met has had different behaviour patterns. Before I can have a reasonably trouble-free relationship with him or her, I have to learn what these patterns are. It is the dogs, in other words, who end up training me.

CHAPTER 6

Kojo's Island

Dear Christine Czajkowski,

My name is Junsuke Ishizu. I am twenty-three years old. Japanese national and member of the wwoof Program. I was excited when I saw your ad. In the wwoof Canada guide . . .

I'm slightly concerned about the food and lodging situation, also, access that how, when, and where should I go into . . . Please assuage my fears in this regard . . .

—Letter from Junsuke Ishizu, spring 2002

I had two Japanese wwoofers that year. The first, along with a Canadian woman, flew in with me after Bucky's moose-chasing adventure, and the two of them stayed at Spinster Lake for ten days. Junsuke Ishizu arrived early in August, some time after the others had gone. He came on a bus-tour plane, sandwiched between two ladies complete with lunch bags, collapsible walking sticks and Tilley hats. Jun's head was shaved and he wore expensive running shoes, cargo pants, four silver earrings around the perimeter of one ear and a single through the other, a hat (not unlike the ladies' hats in shape) made out of crocheted hemp, and a big grin. He spoke strongly accented English, rapidly and with confidence but not always accurately, and introduced himself as *Jun*—the vowel was clipped like the double *o* in *good*. I explained that I would not have much time to talk to him until the end of the day, but showed him his accommodation and where to help himself to the stone-oven bread and beverages I was offering the bus-tour people. Remembering my own years as a world traveller and hitchhiker, I did not doubt that Jun was hungry.

Once the last planeload of visitors had left, I went over to Cabin One to find Jun sitting on the step smoking a cigarette. As so few of my visitors indulge in this habit, I can go months without smelling tobacco (or other inhaled substances) so find the odour very strong at the best of times. These cigarettes were particularly acrid. Jun told me he had spent three months learning English in Calgary and his mother had visited him there and brought the cigarettes over for him; he had found American cigarettes too insipid. I noticed through the open cabin door that two tottering piles of soft cartons, probably forty packets in all, were piled on the bookcase beside a large bottle of vodka. Jun was planning to stay for a month and had obviously made sure he was well supplied with essentials. I thanked him for smoking outside the cabin and found an old tin can for him to use as an ashtray. This was to be Jun's first job as a wwoofer.

He came, he said, from a rural area in Japan. He had grown up in a house with a garden and a dog, which was certainly different from the circumstances of most of the other Japanese nationals I have known, but for all that his knowledge of the countryside was zero. On one occasion I remarked that certain birds had begun to pass through, attracted by the ripening huckleberries. "Birds eat berries?" he said, surprised. Another time I showed him how to catch and clean one of the pan-sized rainbow trout with which my lake is well endowed. A tight mass of some insect or other spilled out of the fish's split belly. "Look at the flies!" I said. "Flies?" he said in horror. (Actually, he said "Fries?") "Fish eat flies?" His face registered such disgust I thought he would never eat a fish again.

Needless to say, Jun's experience with tools matched his knowledge of nature. His first job was to split some firewood. He placed a log round on the chopping block, grasped the axe uncertainly and tapped the sharp end cautiously on the wood. He showed great surprise that the log did not at once fly into several pieces. Granted, firewood at Nuk Tessli is not easy to split. The high altitude distorts and twists the trees, and the short growth spurts mean that a single log round may have more than one ring of knots. Moreover, once I have got a tree down, I do not leave the top to rot as so many firewood gatherers do. I buck it up and bring it home along with the rest. As a result, I have learned to split anything, and I expect my helpers to be able to do the same.

Jun eventually was able to swing an axe along with the best of them, but it took him a fair while to get there. I gave him some pointers—showed him how to look for the weaknesses in a round and to work with the wood, not against it—and left him to it. Poor fellow. He would tap away for about an hour before his grin appeared around the door. "Enough?" he would say. But it never was, and back to the chopping block he had to go.

The clothes he wore when he arrived were too good to ruin with the pitchy, dirty work I expected him to do, so I had him rummage in my spare clothes box to find what he wanted. He lit on a pair of pants that were now too tight for me. They hung like clown pants on his skinny frame, but that was the style of the day, and he thought they were really cool. His hemp hat looked great but was totally unsuitable for this climate. His shaven head was a magnet for bugs, and the large holes in the crocheted fabric gave them plenty of targets to zero in on. So he regretfully put it aside for a baseball cap and a toque. I found him an old Gore-Tex jacket and even gave him a pair of spare hiking boots—they were a bit big, but by stuffing them with extra socks he made them work. His Nike sneakers would have been ruined amongst the bogs and rocks of my backyard.

A couple of clients were already staying at Spinster Lake when Jun arrived, and the day after the bus tour I took all three visitors on a hike to the North Ridge. The trail up there is frequently used so fairly visible at lower elevations, but as we climbed higher and trees suitable for blazing became scarcer, it got increasingly difficult to find the route. I let Jun go in front and explained my marking methods to him, and was pleased to see how quickly he picked up the signs. I would never need to worry about him as long as he was on a marked trail.

However, marked trails were few and far between at Nuk Tessli, and off them, Jun seemed to have no spatial sense whatsoever. The project of the summer was to link my lake—along whose northern shore I had made a trail some years ago—with an old horse route that ran from the head of Cohen Lake (the one above mine) to the final lake upriver, which was hard against the Tweedsmuir Park boundary. It was only a few kilometres west of Nuk Tessli, but even in that short distance, the change in climate was already apparent. Being closer to the coast, it was wetter and different species of birds and plants lived there.

On the first day of our trail building, we canoed to the head of Cohen Lake and I had Jun carry the chainsaw in a backpack so I could cut out the windfalls on the horse trail.

I packed the lunch, an axe and a roll of flagging tape to mark trees as we went along. On the second day we stayed in my lake and worked on the section that would link the two bodies of water. Once he was more at ease in a canoe, this was the part Jun would tackle on his own, and while he lopped branches, I ribboned the route he would be brushing out. On day three we portaged into Cohen Lake again, but this time we parked in the middle. Jun brushed the marked trail back toward my lake, and I determined the route around the last section of the lakeshore.

The scary thing was that even though we headed in the same direction each time and travelled on the same river system, Jun had absolutely no idea that these three areas of work would join up. Each place might have been on a different planet as far as he was concerned. It was the same when he climbed the nearby mountains. He would go up one and have no clue as to which of the others he had already scaled. After the Naomi and Scott fiasco I was terrified to let Jun go far on his own. However, mountain climbing was what he wanted to do. Physically he had an affinity for it, and I wanted him to enjoy as much of it as he could.

In mid-August another client arrived. She was going to fly directly to Wilderness Lake. Jun and I would hike up to meet her, and we would spend two nights in Mary's cabin, then hike down the

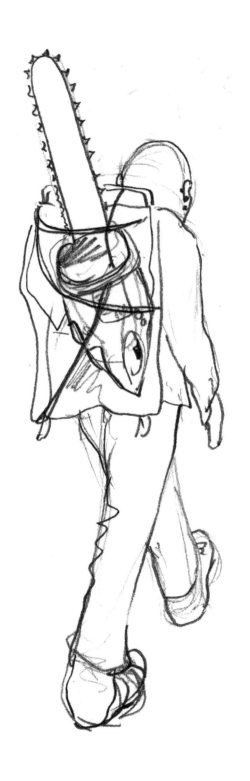

new Wilderness Lake Trail to Nuk Tessli. Jun's only desire, when we went to Wilderness Lake, was to reach the top of Wilderness Mountain. Neither the client nor I had the energy for that—we would content ourselves with a hike to a moraine lake complete with a glacier. I certainly did not want to rob Jun of his summit, but how to explain the danger in terms he would be sure to understand? A ridge provided an obvious route to the top but the weather can never be trusted so far above the treeline, and if the summit socked in, Jun could easily come to grief. I warned him about loose rocks and impressed upon him that he must watch the sky in all directions for clouds moving in. He nodded. He was good at doing what he was told, but I could see that the extent of my concern was not hitting home. Then I had an idea. He was obviously very close to his mother—he had talked a lot about her—so I said, "If you have an accident or get lost, we have to hire a helicopter to look for you.

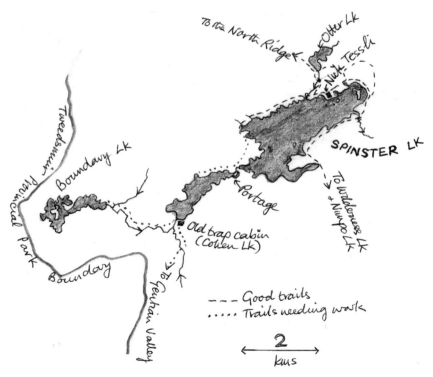

Boundary Lake

Helicopters are very, very expensive. If we need to get a helicopter, your mother will have to pay for it." I didn't know whether this was true, but my point hit home: I could see by his face that he would take the extra needed care. He completed the climb successfully and returned to the cabin safe and sound.

It cannot have been all that easy for Jun to be alone at Nuk Tessli all that time. He was a gregarious person, but I needed time to myself so I often sent him off to work alone. He always did meticulous (if rather slow) work and obviously found a lot of it tedious, but he never complained and always greeted me with his wonderful smile. I found myself becoming quite fond of him. He told me of his friends and family in Japan and showed me pictures of himself and his girlfriend at parties (heavy drinking seemed to be part of their social scene) and his brothers, father and mother. He had even brought along a snap of the dog. His father had died very suddenly not long before Jun had come to Canada and he was evidently still coming to grips with this tragic event.

One morning, when Jun was slated to work alone at the head of the lake, it was extremely windy. Piled plates of lenticular clouds above the mountains indicated that it was going to get worse. Not a day for an inexperienced canoeist who could not swim to be out there. Jun was not naturally an early riser, but he never failed to show up at a reasonable hour, always with his smile in place. That morning I thought I'd go over to his cabin and tell him that as he wouldn't be able to paddle up the lake, he might as well stay in bed a bit longer.

However, he was not sleeping at all. He was praying. He and his family belonged to a Buddhist sect and he meditated morning and evening by chanting a mantra. Among his possessions on the table was a necklace he had been wearing when he had first arrived. The lower end had been tucked into his shirt so I had not been aware of what was attached to the cord. Now I could see that hanging from it was a small leather bag. This was a receptacle for some of his father's ashes. Jun was burying little bits here and there at places he enjoyed. He asked if he could do the same at Nuk Tessli. I was both surprised and flattered that he would consider his experience here worthy of such an honour. If possible, he said, he would like to place them on the top of a mountain.

Jun's great desire was to "learn camping." I had promised him an overnight backpacking trip and I pointed out a small mountain on the edge of The Trench, assured him he had not yet climbed it and asked him if he would like to spend the night out nearby and put his father's ashes on the summit.

The peak was at the head of a wild little alpine valley complete with a roaring snow-fed creek, a glacier and a couple of alpine lakes. It was a favourite destination of mine because the cliffs on the shady side of the valley are permanently moistened by snowmelt running off high cornices, and these encourage an absolutely marvellous collection of rock-alpine plants, many quite rare. There would not be any flowers left by the time we hiked there, but it was a beautiful place. To reach it we would canoe to the head of the next lake upstream, then branch off through trackless bush to the treeline. It would take half a day to get there; in order to climb the peak, we would need to spend two nights camping in the valley.

I figured Jun was not going to "learn camping" if I did all the organizing, so I proposed that we each pack our own food and equipment and also build our own fires and cook our own food. I have never in my life camped without a fire and will do so as long as the country can support it. In one or two spots that I frequently use, I maintain a permanent firepit, but to create that sort of abomination in such a pretty valley as this would be sacrilege. I usually camp in the same place, close to a small lake on a narrow grassy shelf just wide enough for a couple of small tents. The creek's roar fills the ears, the lake is backed by a dense patch of subalpine fir full of dead wood and there are views both up the valley and toward some of the big peaks across The Trench. The lake has a rocky shore and I showed Jun how to roll back some of the stones and place his small fire in the space he had cleared: before we left, the ashes would be well soaked and scattered, and the stones replaced. The proximity of the water would ensure that the fire would not spread, and once we

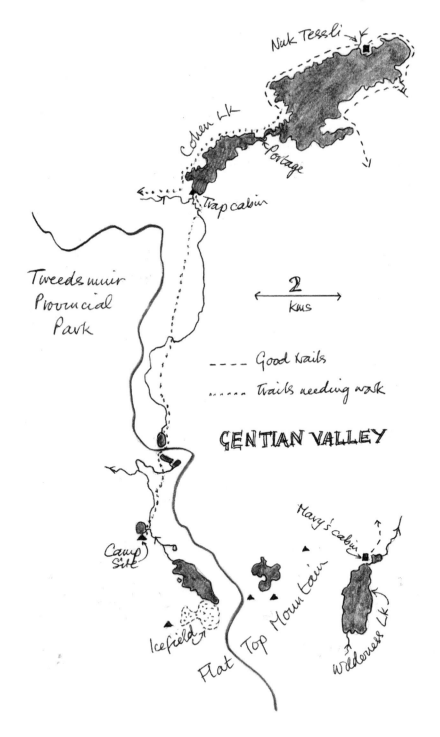

Nuk Tessli

Cohen Lk

Portage

Trap cabin

Tweedsmuir
Provincial
Park

2
kms

- - - - Good trails

· · · · · Trails needing work

GENTIAN VALLEY

Mary's cabin

Camp
Site

Icefield

Flat Top Mountain

Wilderness Lk

had replaced the rocks, it would take a sharp-eyed person to notice that anyone had ever been here.

It was when we made camp that Jun's real initiation into the bush began. Subalpine fir is not the best burning wood. It is difficult to light, and once it is going it burns quickly but without a great deal of heat. But apart from the odd scrub pine some distance away across the valley, subalpine fir was all we had. I showed Jun how to collect the finest dead twigs from the driest part of the bushes and build a pyramid, then place larger sticks in a square around it so they would be in place when the flames took hold. I built my own as an example, then took off my coat and arranged it around the windy side of the pile of twigs, so that when the match was struck, the flame would have some protection. Under my little pyramid of twigs I laid a candle end; candles hold their flames better than matches and their grease helps fuel the blaze. Even in very wet conditions I can make a candle last for many fires. Soon I was drinking tea and my supper was on the boil. Jun had not yet got his fire started. I showed him where he was going wrong—he was using twigs that were too large.

Smoky campfire

After several more tries he was able to start it, but it died and went out. An hour later, after a great deal of puffing and blowing, his eyes were red and swollen from the smoke.

In the end, I relented and made him some tea but insisted he cook his own food. Eventually he managed it, and over the next two days each subsequent fire took a little less time until he was able to cook his last breakfast in less than half an hour.

The weather gods decided to make Jun's camping experience one he would remember. There was to be no enjoyable lazing around the campfire while the sun set over the Coast Range that first night, for just after Jun finished eating it started to rain. It was not yet dark, but we dived for our tents and there we remained until well into the following day. The rain pounded and the wind roared. Mine is a tough little four-season tent, but it has seen a lot of hard use and a drip started above my forehead. I deflected it by running my finger from it down the side of the tent, but after a while there was another cold splat on my face and the drip started up again. At first light I made a dash for a hunk of bread (I always hang food in the dog packs close to the fire area and well away from the tents), but it was not until mid-morning that the rain eased and I crawled out into the sodden world. Jun appeared to be asleep but I shook his tent until I heard a groan, then warned him that if he did not cook some food now, he might not get a chance later. So we went through our fire routine again. We had stored kindling in our tents, but all the larger wood was rain-soaked. Nonetheless, Jun managed to cook his food in slightly less time than he had done the night before.

The clouds began to break apart a little, and there were even occasional patches of blue sky. But the storm was far from over and the wind had increased. Violently gusty around our tents, it roared like an express train above our heads. The peak Jun wanted to climb was totally hidden in vapour and I didn't doubt that the winds at that altitude would be hurricane force and snow would be falling. It was far too dangerous for him to attempt the ascent. He could either find a spot near here to bury his father's ashes, or take them back to Nuk Tessli.

A hike around the side of the mountain seemed worth a try, however. The same ancient ice age that had smoothed the Charlotte Alplands plateaus had left a wide shelf of land on each side of The Trench. These were mostly above the treeline, but they sloped into the upper part of the forest, so the bottom of The Trench was hidden by trees. However, by following the shelf around the mountain we would reach a shallow saddle that in good weather would give us spectacular views. How much we would be able to see in this wild weather was debatable, but I thought we might as well do something with our day.

We walked around the small lake in front of our tents and skirted the large snow patch that lay beside it. At once we were confronted with a wind so strong we could barely make headway. Sometimes we stumbled over tundra and at other times we slithered on rockslides and boulders. Monarch, on our right, remained encased in angry swirling grey, but other peaks played hide-and-seek with clouds that would one minute pound us with stinging snow pellets and the next break apart to reveal sudden and startling gleams of sun. The interplay of black cloud and shadow, spotlight sun and glimpses of freshly whitened buttresses and peaks, all appearing and fading rapidly as the wind flung vapour onto the peaks one moment and ripped it apart the next, was nature at its most dramatic.

Just below the saddle, I turned around so I could adjust some clothing with my back to the wind, and saw my two dogs fighting furiously. Max had the ripped and bloody carcass of a young marmot in his mouth.

The marmot must have been weak or sick, or very foolish: it was only the second time in all those years that I had seen the dogs catch one of these animals. I could see the dogs snarling and biting and leaping at each other, but I could hear nothing because of the wind. The silent, violent battle seemed very strange.

Suddenly, Bucky broke away and ran toward me. He clung to my heel as if he would never leave my side again. Then Max came over, too, the dead marmot hanging from his jaws. Bucky must have finally learned something, because every time Max changed his position in relation to me, Bucky moved as well, making very sure I was always exactly in between. Max packed the marmot around for a while but then went off and buried it among some rocks.

The storm blew itself out during the night and the morning was limpid and dead calm. Early sun warmed us, but clouds filtered in and it started to rain before we arrived home. Jun now had only a few days left at Spinster Lake and he still had to find a place to bury the last of his father's ashes. He took the canoe to several vantage points on the lake and eventually chose the exposed end of the island where the tree swallows nest. From there he could see the cabin, the lake, the principal view of Monarch and Migma, his work area and all the summits he had climbed. I watched him go over and build his tiny cairn, his young body darkly silhouetted against the dancing sunlit water. As he completed his little ceremony, a wind-distorted chant came to me across the waves.

Jun cried when he left. "My father's name is Kojo," he said

Marmot

as we hugged on the dock before he stepped onto the plane. "Will you think of him sometimes so that he doesn't get lonely?" It was hardly the kind of thing I had expected when I applied to become a wwoofer host. But think of him I do. Kojo's Island lies in front of the bay window. I watch the sun rise over it on the shortest day and travel east as the year slides slowly into spring. Many other wwoofers have since come to Spinster Lake, and their legacies have all become part of its small history.

CHAPTER 7

Snowshoes and Spotted Dick

Very wild wind. SSW. +6°C. The cabin trembles in the worst gusts. The sky is clear, the stars huge like lamps. They seem to tremble, as if they are having trouble hanging onto their places: no doubt it is the refraction caused by the violently disturbed air, causing much the same effect as images seen through heat waves, but it seems as though the stars are on the verge of being wrenched from their roots and flung across the heavens.

Most of the snow has been licked up: by flashlight it looks as though there are only 15 centimetres out there, half of what there was when I arrived. It's totally rotten. I had to put the snowshoes on to get to the outhouse.

(later)

Cloud patches overhead are ripping off from the dark mass that hides Monarch and Co. The wind has lessened—probably only gale force now. Floyd is supposed to come in with an important package in a few days but I dread to think what the lake is like. Pools of wind-ruffled water lie all over it—I hope they are only on the surface, but there are a lot of open spots near the rocks along the shore. John Edwards was talking on the radiophone last night. He commented on the storm. He would be getting even worse winds down at Lonesome Lake as The Trench would funnel them even more efficiently. There's open water on his lake, too.

I'm supposed to phone Mary tonight and tell her what the ice conditions are like so she can pass the message on to Floyd, but I daren't even go out there to look.

—Journal, January 6, 2003

At the end of 2001, three of my four books were either out of print or almost there. One publisher had gone belly up and another no longer published books in my genre, which was billed as adult non-fiction. It was a bad time for the publishing industry, which was still recovering from a devastating merger between two large bookselling chains, so no one was taking on anything new. This circumstance coincided with an increase in the Land Office's fees from $1,500 to $5,000 in one jump, so I was having a very hard time making ends meet. I had not stopped writing—creativity is a craving, like a drug—and I had several unpublished manuscripts in various stages of preparation: *Lonesome: Memoirs of a Wilderness Dog*, the story of my wilderness life as seen through the eyes of my first canine companion; *Gentian Violet*, a murder mystery that had so far received upward of thirty rejections; and *Snowshoes and Spotted Dick: Letters From a Wilderness Dweller*, an account of the years spent building Cabin Three.

In 2002, the literary side of my life at last began to look more hopeful. First a German publisher expressed interest in translating *Cabin at Singing River*, the story of my life at Lonesome Lake. Negotiations, however, progressed very slowly. I received the contract early in the year but the promised advance, which was supposed to arrive in July, became entangled in the most amazing bureaucratic claptrap and did not actually materialize until the following January. Shortly afterwards, the English version of the same book was reissued by Raincoast Books. Things were starting to look up. The general consensus regarding the murder mystery was that it probably wouldn't go anywhere unless I could prove that I could write several more in a series. I had plenty of ideas, but so far, no time. A publisher had also expressed interest in Lonesome's story, but although the managing editor kept saying that a contract would arrive in the next mail, nothing happened;

this same nothing continued to happen for two whole years so I eventually took it away from her. It is not considered ethical for a writer to send a manuscript to a second publisher while the first is still considering it, so while *Lonesome* languished in Vancouver I could do nothing about interesting anyone else. If publishers care about the fact that an author has no chance of gaining income from a manuscript that is sitting at the bottom of their "to do" pile, they don't show it.

Then, while I was on a book tour down the Coast in the fall, I received a contract from Harbour Publishing for *Snowshoes and Spotted Dick*. After some negotiating, the publisher agreed to schedule it for October 2003, which was great news indeed, as usually a publisher plans ahead for two years and a manuscript must wait for at least that long before it gets into the bookstores. A day before I was due to leave the Coast and head back north, Harbour phoned to ask whether they could bring the book forward to spring, as the manuscript would not need a lot of work and one of the books originally scheduled for that slot was proving too difficult to get off the ground in time.

My last book had been a spring release, and in my experience, they never sell as well, at least initially, so I was not as pleased as I might have been. Also, a spring book barely gave me time to organize a decent book tour—some venues require bookings a year ahead. But I was so thankful to get some money in the bank that I agreed. There were, however, two problems to surmount. One was that the electronic copy of the manuscript (which all publishers demand these days) had been produced on my old Mac Classic, whose program was so "ancient," it would not be easy to convert to a readable form for the publisher's computers. Fortunately I managed to get back to Nimpo just before the Anahim school closed for the Christmas break, and Dianne Chamberlain, a teacher who ran the library and the computer room, was able to do the necessary work.

The other problem involved the editing process. No author can produce a book without input from an objective reader. The author is too close to it. A good editor will say: "This is more effective than that—why don't you put it first." Or, as is often the case with my work, "City people have difficulty in visualizing this. Please describe a 'peavey.'" The manuscript must travel back and forth between the editor and author several times. I very much enjoy working with a good editor as I feel I am learning a great deal—and I don't have to pay for a course, or sit in a classroom in a city, to do it! Harbour's production manager kept saying how tight the time frame would be even under normal circumstances, but we had the added problem of getting proofs back and forth to Nuk Tessli in the middle of winter, a time when I often don't receive mail for long periods. I made arrangements to stagger my freight deliveries instead of having them all at once. Floyd would bring in the first edited draft in early January, and he would come in again to pick it up after I had added my comments, a process that was expected to take about a week. A month down the road, another draft of the manuscript would have to travel back and forth in the same way.

After the fall book tour, I was, as usual, anxious to get back into the mountains as soon as possible. Floyd was away but I managed to badger someone else into putting skis on his plane, and I flew home during Christmas week. The fall had been extremely mild and the ice was barely good enough. Nimpo Lake had been snowless and smooth as glass, and when we flew over my lake, it was to see somewhat ominous grey patches dotting much of the snowy surface. It was to be hoped that these were simply water stains and not weak spots. We landed without mishap, but when I cut my water hole the following day I was alarmed to see that there were only 15 centimetres of ice. This is no problem to walk on, but pilots normally like 20 centimetres to be on the safe side.

Forty-eight hours after I arrived home, a mega-thaw began. Hot winds pounded us for several days. When it finally began to freeze again at night, a second skin of ice formed over the standing water. Eventually I put on snowshoes (simply to distribute weight: there was no snow left on the ice) and shuffled cautiously onto the lake, chopping holes with an axe to check the depth as I went. Within the circle of islands, the ice was just 20 centimetres deep, but out on the open lake it was thicker—which was odd, because when it freezes, the water within the protection of the islands gels before that out on the windier open lake. Anyway, I could radiophone Mary and tell her to pass on the message that the ice was now adequate for Floyd to bring the manuscript.

A lot of people were involved in getting that document back and forth between the editor and myself. Madeira Park on the Sunshine Coast, where the publishing company is located, is a ferry ride from Vancouver. The manuscript had to be sent by courier from Madeira Park to the Vancouver airport, placed with Pacific Coastal Airlines, which runs the daily charter to Anahim Lake, picked up by Mary and delivered to Floyd, who then flew it in to me. For this to run smoothly, all of us had to know what was going on: it was a perfect job for Rosemary Neads and her internet access. The publisher's production manager emailed Rosemary to tell her the manuscript had been dispatched. Rosemary phoned Mary so she could be ready to meet the scheduled flight at 10:00 a.m. the next day, and Mary called me on the radiophone that evening to alert me that if things went as planned, Floyd would be in the following afternoon. I specifically needed to know this, as Bucky had added plane chasing to his repertoire. In summer he contented himself with teetering on the edge of the dock when planes came in, but in winter, at the first sound of an aircraft, he ran eagerly onto the ice, taking no notice of my screams and yells. Given the chance, he would run in front of the aircraft and try to bite it, putting himself in great danger from the prop and risking damage to the aircraft as well.

Once all this was set in motion the only restriction would be the weather, but fortunately there were no more thaws, the winter remained mild, sunny and relatively snowless, and all the planned flight days were perfect. When the package was ready to be returned, I radiophoned Mary to contact Floyd so that he could fly in to pick it up. Mary delivered the package to the airport and land-phoned Rosemary; she emailed the editor; Pacific Coastal Airlines took the manuscript to Vancouver and placed it with the courier, and we were in business. Many city folk don't understand how life can function without a phone—not everyone would have taken on this cumbersome form of communication with such equanimity. But the publisher had grown up as the child of a gyppo logger and was used to life far from amenities. Those of us who live out here have no problem making such a system work. I later asked the production manager if she had been nervous about the deadlines, and she said that my book had been one of the easiest to deal with during that season.

The manuscript flights brought freight and mail, and among the letters was the second part of my advance for *Snowshoes and Spotted Dick* and, finally, the overdue advance from Germany, which was paid in euros. I prepared a letter to the bank while Floyd waited for me so that I could mail the cheques right away. Suddenly I had more money in my account than since I had started my wilderness life nearly twenty years before. It wouldn't last long: there were bills to pay and I had a wish list as long as my arm, but it gave me a great feeling of relief.

There was no freight to bring in on the second two flights so Rosemary, who loves flying, came along for the ride. She had never been to Nuk Tessli before. To save her the hour-long snow-machine ride out from The Precipice, Floyd went there to pick her up—Float Plane Lake in their valley is just long enough for a small aircraft to land on. It was a great treat to have a visitor. Floyd, unfortunately, could not spare more than an hour, but Rosemary and I managed to get an awful lot of talking done during that time. It was a

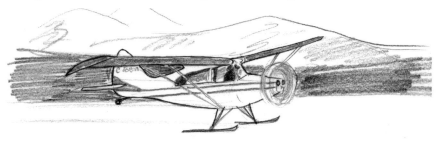

Floyd's plane

spectacularly gorgeous day. Rosemary had recently acquired a new toy—a digital camera—and she delightedly took snaps of the plane and the views, including one looking through the window toward Mount Monarch. When she emailed the production manager to tell her that the manuscript was on its way, she sent some of the snaps. The publisher pounced on one of them, saying it was exactly what he wanted for the cover of the book. I thought it very fitting that Rosemary, who was now heavily embroiled in my business life, should be so honoured.

CHAPTER 8

The Sardine Cure

"Do you have trouble with wolves?" asked a man who was attending one of my slide shows.

"No, I never have trouble with wolves," I replied. "I see them sometimes, and their tracks are all over the place, winter and summer, but they've never been a bother."

"But you must have trouble with wolves!" the man insisted.

—Conversation at a slide show, fall 2001

Dear Nick,

Here's a Chilcotin story for you. I am assured, by the people who told it to me, that it is perfectly true!

A few years back, there was a move afoot to poison wolves on the Chilcotin. At a heated meeting, the ranchers said they were losing too many cows. (They maintain it is easy to spot a wolf kill, as the carcass is scattered and no other animal does that; they also maintain that wolves will not eat carrion. But I have twice come across instances where wolves ate dead animals—one, a bear that had been shot by the trapper, had been dead two years.)

Be that as it may, the poisoners were adamant that wolves were the prime cause of their cow losses. A man with a more humane attitude got up and said that in the Yukon experiments had been made with immunosterilants that would effectively prevent the wolves from breeding. Maybe that was a better way to approach the matter.

At this, one of the ranchers leapt to his feet and said, "Them damn wolves are eating my cows, not f—king them!"
—Letter to Nick Berwian, February 28, 2003

I awoke one February night to a muffled snapping and snarling, much the same noise that Bucky makes when Max is lying in front of his kennel and preventing him from getting into it. "Let them sort it out," I thought to myself sleepily. But the sound was repeated, this time for much longer, and I realized it was coming not from the porch where the kennels are, but from the ice.

I reached for my glasses (which were, for once, where I could find them) and stared out of the bay window. It was a mild night, cloudy, windless, no moon and no stars, but wilderness nights are rarely pitch black and the pale blanket of snow on the lake backlit some activity close to a group of rocks not far from the shore. There appeared to be four animals having some kind of a scuffle. Bucky's dark form was easily distinguished, but the other three animals were lighter and harder to focus on. One must be Max, but I could not be sure of the identity of the others. Obviously some kind of dog, but they were too big for foxes. There are plenty of coyotes at Nimpo Lake; I've never seen or heard them up here, but because of the low snow level they might have strayed out of their usual territory. I grabbed a flashlight, thrust my feet into snow boots and ran out onto the deck. The strangers took off at once and the dogs came up to me grinning and panting and wagging and looking enormously pleased with themselves. The flashlight beam just touched one of the retreating animals, which turned and looked at me for a moment, its eyes twin green coals in a pale face, before disappearing into the darkness. It was chilly standing there in my underwear and I figured that was the end of it so I went back to bed.

I don't know how long I was asleep but I surfaced to hear the snarling once again. This time it was a little farther up the lake and I could see nothing through the windows. I pulled on outer clothes this time and went down onto the ice. Once again I thought I saw green eyes at the limit of the flashlight beam but could not get a good look at the owners; however, I went to the site of the first scrap and checked out the tracks. There had been about a centimetre of snow the previous day so the footprints were clear, though they had been much scuffed by the skirmish. Bucky's smaller footmarks stood out; the other animals' prints were all about the same size, which would indicate they had been made by wolves. I don't see them very often, but wolves are very much part of the landscape here. They frequently travel back and forth between Whitton Creek and the game trail that

leads down to The Trench. Their tracks cross the head of my lake and run down the series of meadows where Bucky and Max chased the moose. When they are running normally, a wolf's track is much rounder than a dog's, but because of the scuffling it was difficult to tell them apart.

It was only then that I became aware that Max was not trotting happily around with Bucky. He was walking toward me with great difficulty, apparently badly hurt. I could not see much blood, and Max's dense, springy winter coat hid his injuries, but he was severely distressed, gasping and staring, and he could barely climb up the little trail to the cabin.

I found an old coat for him to lie on and brought him inside. He at once lay down and stretched out and gradually his breathing returned to normal. It was very hot inside the cabin as I had baked bread that morning and the stones of the oven radiated heat like a furnace. After a while Max got up and stood with his nose by the door so I let him out, thinking he was finding the heat too much. He must have needed to relieve himself, because he walked along the trail past the outhouse to where he usually poops in winter. He was gone quite a while and returned in a state of great agony. Once more I brought him in, but this time he couldn't lie down—every time he tried to lower himself he yelped and straightened up again. Such blood as there was seemed to be around his rear end, but when I tried to move his tail to have a look, he cried most piteously. Eventually I was able to view his injuries. His anus had been badly chewed. There was another wound in the dense fur above his tail—the wolf must have got hold of him right at the root of his tail and hung on. If I had not gone out when I did, he would surely have been killed.

There wasn't a great deal I could do for him. Human drugs are often fatal to animals, so although I had some (rather ancient) human painkillers, I did not dare give them to Max. A vet was out of the question, at least in the middle of the night, because the local planes cannot fly in the dark. But even when daylight came, to reach a vet I would have had to pack all my freezeables in the root cellar and then hire two planes to get me and both dogs to Nimpo, drive four hours to Williams Lake, then do the trip in reverse to get home. Even slightly more affluent than usual, that kind of expense was far beyond my means.

I made a bed for the dog out of old rugs and blankets in the porch—he would not be able to duck into his kennel—and kept him supplied with drinking water and whatever food he wanted to eat, which wasn't much. He had always been a picky eater, but now even treats like canned dog food and cookies did not interest him. The location of the wound meant there was a very strong risk of infection; I had a few old dog penicillin tablets and gave them to him morning and night in a treat.

For the next three days, Max barely moved. Once or twice he walked to his bathroom spot, always leaving slowly but steadily, and coming back in agony. On the fourth evening his eyes were sunk and his nose dry. He was often a bit constipated in normal times and if he was bothered by that, his injury certainly wouldn't be helping matters. So for supper that night I gave him a can of sardines. He licked up every last bit.

The next morning he was gone from the porch. Worried, I ran along the trail past the outhouse, wondering if he had crawled away to die. No sign of him there, and my next thought was that the sardines might have made him thirsty. The temperature had been slightly cooler that night and his water bowl was frozen. My bucket was empty so I walked onto the ice to chop open the water hole. And there was Max, several hundred metres out on the ice with Bucky. When he saw me, he actually loped toward me, eager, no doubt, for his pill-laden treat. He even managed to wag his poor, ravaged tail.

CHAPTER 9

And Now We'll Relax.
With Max.

A funny thing.

Right after sunrise, a few days after I had returned from the 2003 spring book tour, Bucky barked somewhere out of sight northwest of the cabin and shortly afterwards came home very wet. Max (who was by now fully recovered from his wolf adventure) seemed uninterested, so I assumed Bucky had been chasing ducks. He had suddenly discovered that he could swim, and now anything he saw on the water necessitated an instant plunge in that direction: he never learned how easily he would be outmanoeuvred in that element.

Some time later I heard him bark again. A bit of a wind was blowing by that time and the sound was less distinct, but it occurred to me that it had been in the back of my consciousness for some time. When he was not tied up, Bucky rarely barked; I figured the most likely scenario was that he had treed a bear. I took the bear spray, called Max and went cautiously toward the noise, thinking to try and catch Bucky and bring him home . . .

—Journal, June 8, 2003

The trail in that direction went past Cabin One and then across a bog I have called Cabin Meadow. When I first came to Nuk Tessli, huge snowdrifts would still be there in early June, but this year only a few dirty piles were left among the brown and waterlogged sedges. Willow twigs were in bud but did not yet bear leaves. The flower buds—the "pussy willows"—were tight and silvery; even they had not fully opened yet. Nothing seemed to be moving and Bucky was invisible at that point, but then he obligingly barked again and showed me where to look. Hidden until I stepped away from the trees was a large cow moose. She was losing her winter fur in scrofulous patches but seemed otherwise fit and well fleshed; she was feeding in a thicket of willow bushes whose tops barely tickled her belly.

The strange thing was, even after Max and I stepped into view, she did not run away. She stared at us but seemed unconcerned—even Bucky and his yapping were only minor irritants to her. She occasionally laid her ears back and lunged at him, otherwise she munched placidly and periodically licked her lips with her remarkable tongue.

I had not realized before what an immense organ that is. The

mouth, for a start, is huge. The bulbous nose is familiar enough, but when the jaws are open, they gape like a cartoon mouth and take up half the moose's head. The tongue is so long that the cow would have been able to wiggle the prehensile tip in her ear had she been so inclined. As it was, she curled it around bunches of the stubby willow twigs and hauled them into that extraordinary maw.

Why didn't she flee? Did she have a calf hidden in the bushes? I didn't think it wise to investigate. Bucky refused to come when I called, and I knew I wouldn't be able to catch him even if I dared go close enough to the moose to do so. The only thing was to let nature take its course. Max had shown some interest when the moose lunged at Bucky, but while she was feeding he ignored her, and he returned to the cabin with me. Bucky's yapping persisted on and off for half the day; when he eventually got tired of it and came home I tied him up at once and kept him on a lead for a couple of days, but the moose did not come back into the meadow. Days later I saw her picking her way through the shallows on the far side of the lake, and found what were probably her tracks on and off throughout the summer. But at no time did I see the slightest indication that she had a calf.

That made her behaviour even odder.

Snowshoes and Spotted Dick was launched on April 22 at the downtown Vancouver Public Library. There were two things I did not know when I picked the date: one was that Margaret Atwood, arguably Canada's most famous contemporary author, was launching *Oryx and Crake* in Vancouver that same evening, and the other was that a hockey game was also scheduled that night. For those with a literary bent, Margaret Atwood would be hard to pass up—if I'd only known in time, I would have gone to hear her speak myself. I doubt many of my followers would have been interested in the hockey game—despite the fact that the Vancouver Canucks were on an unprecedented winning streak—but the arena was just down the road from the library and parking would be a nightmare. After the game, hockey fans might well present some interesting driving complications due to their euphoria or gloom, depending on how the game went. Consequently my audience was smaller than I had hoped.

Still, I had another couple of venues in the Lower Mainland that were more lucrative, then crossed to Vancouver Island, where I gave six slide shows without a break. This would have been tiring enough by itself, but thanks to Harbour Publishing's aggressive promotion efforts, they were interspersed by several media appearances. I spoke in Victoria, Shawnigan Lake, Duncan, Nanaimo, Campbell River and Courtenay. Slide shows are fun—they give me a wonderful excuse to show off—but they are exhausting and I am not capable of driving very far after them. After Duncan I had to be at Nanaimo, over an hour's drive away, for a TV show by 6:50 a.m. the following morning. Travelling at night was not an option for me, so I had to get up at about four to give myself time to walk the dogs and have a breakfast before I got on the road. After the interview I had to twiddle my thumbs in Nanaimo all day, waiting to perform there that night, but then had to be in Campbell River over two hours' drive away for a radio interview early the following day. And that is how it went.

The Nanaimo TV show turned out to be something a bit unexpected. Generally for these events I am told to arrive between ten and twenty minutes beforehand, then I am interviewed for two to fifteen minutes if it is live and maybe half an hour if it is taped (and edited), and then I am shown the door.

The interview in Nanaimo was a little different. It was on *New Day*, which was put out by New VITV (now known as "A-Channel Vancouver Island"). The first odd thing about it was the studio. It was not a dark and windowless room, as is usually the case. One side was all glass and it faced a brick patio on which was parked a van with Emergency Response Team written on the side. Next to it was deposited a large rectangular block of ice. Inside the studio was a small, round table at which I was told to sit, with my back to the patio, and a couch. This piece of furniture was specifically for visiting dogs, but Max was too big for it and had to lie down on the floor. Near him was a huge brand-new chainsaw attached to an Alaskan

Mill, much larger but otherwise identical to the rig I had used to cut all the heavy lumber at Nuk Tessli. Across the room, which was wedge-shaped, was a counter spread with cooking equipment watched over by a nervous young man who wore an apron and hat emblazoned with the words "Dairy Queen." Above his head hung a series of TV monitors; the news and advertisements were being put together in another room.

Our host was a man called Bruce Williams. A few minutes after 7:00 a.m. he walked in, followed by a second man shouldering a large video camera—not quite as big as the one used by the *Great Canadian Rivers* crew, but it must have been a fair weight to pack around.

The monitors were showing a picture of Nanaimo, and a female voice happily told everyone what a gorgeous day it was out there. Suddenly we were on the air. Clutching a hand-held microphone, Bruce interviewed the Dairy Queen fellow for about three minutes. Then he talked briefly to me while I held up the new book, gestured to the cameraman to include Max in a shot, mentioned the chainsaw shop and walked outside to the thawing ice block and the Emergency Response Team vehicle, his soft-footed cameraman trailing behind him. A man with a small chainsaw started carving the ice block. He was advertising an ice-cutting competition that was to be held the following weekend at Qualicum Beach—this in a climate that rarely gets frost or snow even in the middle of winter, and it was the end of April already!

I figured that was it but stayed put, waiting to be told I could go, for I did not want to make an unnecessary noise at the wrong time. But lo and behold, after another burst of news, weather and ads, Bruce did the round of interviews, with variations, again. This pattern was repeated over and over again for the next two hours. It was like a party. Soon we were laughing and joking, and eating the delicious hamburgers that the Dairy Queen fellow was preparing. The only one who was not at all animated was Max. He was a TV veteran by then, but he always finds studio lights too hot and soon stretched flat out on his side, fast asleep. Just before the end of each of the live sessions, Bruce got the cameraman to focus on the dog and said, "And now we'll relax. With Max."

At one point we were all outside clutching our hamburgers and watching the ice carver deftly creating the next stage of his sculpture (which turned out to be a Canucks emblem: given the euphoria about the Canucks' recent and unusual successes, what else could it be?) when two men wheeling bicycles approached us. They were no longer young, had American accents and were towing little bicycle trailers: it appeared they had ridden all the way up from California.

The eldest was probably close to sixty. "I'm looking for Charlie," he said.

"There's no Charlie here," replied our interviewer. "My name is Bruce."

"I was told to ask for Charlie," said the American. "We're looking for some breakfast."

"Oh, you mean Charlie's Restaurant. It's just along the road there. It might not be open yet." Bruce looked at his watch. "Give it another ten minutes."

"Fer Chrissake," growled the older American, beginning to get cranky. "It's nearly 8:30 and there's nowhere to get breakfast yet? What kind of a town is this?"

Bruce decided he had better calm things down. "You do realize this is a live TV show." He gestured to the camera. "You're on the air right now."

At which the cyclist turned and faced right into the wide lens hood of the camera and said, very deliberately, "Get that f---ing thing out of here!"

Everyone's jaw dropped. Bruce, of course, affected shock and quickly smoothed the whole thing over, but I could see that he, like the rest of us, was secretly delighted. "Live" shows usually run a seven-second delay before the material is actually aired—that's why you hear the bleeps—but the incident was so unexpected that I wondered whether the censor had been quick enough to block it out.

It was certainly the most entertaining interview in which I have ever had the privilege to participate.

The ice was late going out that year, which was a real surprise because the winter had been so mild and snowless. Successive layers of frozen overflow constitute the greater portion of the ice on my lake, and by the end of winter it might be a metre thick. But there was no rhyme or reason for a mild, low-snow winter to relinquish its ice so reluctantly. I have known my lake to be open as early as May 17 and try to arrive at Nimpo by the middle of that month so I can be ready to go home the minute it is possible to fly in.

But in the middle of May that year, there was fresh ice in the bay in front of Mary's resort, and the local pilots were only just exchanging their skis for floats. As soon as they had them on, some neighbours of Mary's went for a tootle around—and came back with the startling news that the roof of the Wilderness Lake cabin had blown off. It had been flown up there only three years before. The roof must have gone during the wild, warm storms we had at the beginning of January, as that valley was directly aligned with the winds we had then. Mary's neighbour took her up in his plane to see the cabin. Wilderness Lake was still frozen and would stay that way for another month; as the plane had floats on, it could not land. There was no sign of the roof at all: it was presumed buried in the huge snowdrift that lay behind the building. Mary kindly asked her pilot to take a turn around Nuk Tessli to check on my cabins; from the air, everything appeared to be all right.

Metal, fibreglass insulation, strapping, tarpaper, everything had gone, as Mary learned in July, when the ice went out and she was finally able to check out the cabin. The debris, when it eventually emerged from the snow, was found to be scattered for hundreds of metres behind the building. Amazingly, however, there was very little damage inside: the rafters and the ceiling boards they supported were still in place and almost no water had dribbled through. As soon as they were able to land, the mess was cleaned up and a new roof was put on, but I was quite amused to see, when I walked up there later in the summer with some wwoofers, that for some considerable distance around the cabin, the round grass nests that the mice make for their summer homes stood out like beacons—they were all bright balls of fluffy yellow fibreglass.

But that was later. On May 30, Floyd flew over my lake and told me that there was not even a hole big enough to land in at the upper end, where the flow from the incoming river opens it first. He reckoned it would be about a week before anyone could get in there. It had been sunny but quite cold and frosty at nights; what we needed was wind.

I whiled away some of my spare time by going down to The Precipice. Since Rosemary had been handling my email, I tried to visit every time I passed through Nimpo. I would spend two days solid on her computer in an attempt to organize my business life so that things would run as smoothly as possible when I was back in the bush.

On the weekend I went down there, the spring cattle drive was taking place. The rancher who occupied the middle of the valley was moving his cows up to their summer grazing, and various friends came down with their horses to help, turning the chore into a big party. There was always a barbecue and homemade music around a big fire—it was one of the few chances I had to socialize with the people I considered my neighbours.

The rest of my Nimpo time was spent matting and pricing artwork for the fall book tour, and packing what I would need for a trip to Williams Lake at the end of June. I hated to go out from Spinster Lake during the summer—a trip outside wasted so much time. Consequently I was fretting even more at the delay, because I would have only three weeks alone before I had to be out again. On June 3, one of Duncan Stewart's pilots sent me the message that the top half of my lake was open. I booked a plane for the 5th, knowing that I would at least be able to get onto the water even if the ice still hung around the islands and blocked the passage into the cabins. If that was the case, I would have to stash the freight and fetch it home by canoe, but in fact, although ragged sheets of ice were still piled on the windward side of the land masses, getting into the wharf was no problem.

June is my month. I need it to recover from the stress of being outside for so long and to prepare both physically and mentally for the influx of summer visitors. Some summers I manage to stay in for the whole four and a half months without a break (I go out just in time for The Precipice Thanksgiving party), but this year at the end of June I prepared for the scheduled hike to the road. Because I had flown in, my truck was not at the Forestry campground at Charlotte Lake, but Mary kindly agreed to meet me there two days after I set off.

It was a dull morning that looked by the clouds as though it was going to get windy quite soon, so I wanted to leave in good time. Canoeing to the trailhead against the wind is no fun at all. To make sure that Bucky didn't meet anything he wanted to chase en route, I decided against having the dogs run along the shore, and put them both in the boat. Bucky had been coerced into it only once before, so it was not without misgivings that I coaxed the two dogs aboard and eased myself in with them. We travelled in what I call the barge, an ugly brute of a boat that is hard to paddle but has the advantage of being very stable. I was expecting to bring four wwoofers home with me so I towed an extra canoe behind and carried our packs in it. If we tipped over, at least our gear would stay dry. It is a slow way to make progress but as long as the wind is not too strong, it is not difficult.

The wind began to pick up just as I arrived at the trailhead so

I gave myself a pat on the back for having done that right and, with Bucky on his lead, climbed up toward Octopus Lake. We had almost reached the bridge when Max suddenly showed extreme interest in a scent and started to run excitedly back and forth. Bucky was going mad, yelling and pulling, but there was no way I was going to let him go. I tried to grab Max as he ran by, but all I got was a handful of disappearing tail. Next thing, he was furiously biting at something, then rearing back and frantically wiping his face with his paws before trying to grab the creature again. Oh, no! There was only one animal likely to cause that kind of reaction. In twenty years I had seen only three indications that porcupines inhabit this territory: the distinctive and curious tracks in a dried pond one September in the alpine, a tuft of bear hair full of quills on the trail out to Charlotte Lake (I wouldn't have liked to meet *that* guy) and a comparatively benign encounter that another of my dogs had some distance away and many years before.

I tied Bucky to a tree and ran for Max. Maddened by the porcupine, he tried to evade me, but I managed to pull him off. The porcupine was quite small, not much bigger than a large cat, so must have been a young one. It was curled into a ball with all its spines bristling and seemed unhurt.

Max, however, was in a horrifying state. About a hundred quills bristled from his jaws, his legs and the front of his packs.

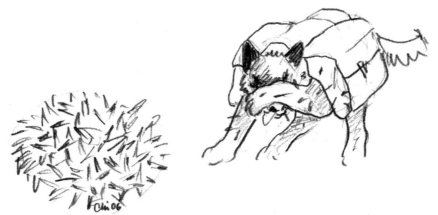

Max and the porcupine

Frothy blood poured from his mouth and his protruding tongue was covered in quills, but I could not see how far down his throat they had gone. This was not an injury he was going to recover from by himself, or one that I could deal with alone. Walking to meet Mary at the Forestry campground was out of the question. I would have to charter a plane. But first I had to get Max home. I begged, pulled and cajoled him back to the canoe; it took twice as long as the journey up because he kept wanting to sit down and rest. It was now quite windy. I still wanted to leave at least one boat at the trailhead ready for when I hiked home again with the wwoofers, so I took a chance and put all of us together with our packs into the barge. Surfing on the waves, we blew back to the cabin.

No one seemed to be listening on the radiophone, but eventually the woman who operates the office at the airport heard me and picked up. She checked with both float-plane companies; Stewarts said that not only could they get in within the hour but also they would give me a cheap rate, as they would be on their way home from another charter.

Fortunately there was not a lot for me to do at Nimpo: I had used some of my time waiting for the ice to prepare for the Williams Lake trip. So I threw what I needed into the truck and drove straight to the vet's. Max had calmed down and was able to close his mouth by this point so I knew he could breathe all right, but he refused to drink, and after the trauma, the hike home, the wait for the plane ride and four hours of hyperventilating in the truck, he must have been very dehydrated. Despite my early start that morning, it was after business hours by the time we arrived at Williams Lake, so on top of the flight and the vet fees I was charged extra for that.

Max was no longer making me feel very relaxed.

CHAPTER 10

A Queendom of One

Dear Nick,

As you liked the wolf one so much, here's another Chilcotin story for you!

When I was waiting at the wharf at Nimpo one time, I heard a bunch of pilots swapping yarns. One described how he had flown the offspring of a well-known local pioneer; they wanted to scatter their father's ashes over the country where he had ranched. The thing you have to know about this pioneer is that he was renowned for not paying his bills.

The plane took off, and when they reached the ranch, one of the side windows was pushed open. The pilot was just about to tell his passengers to wait until he banked the plane around so that they would not be fighting the wind, but too late. The lid of the urn was pulled off, and the ashes all blew back into the aircraft.

"That guy owed me money all the time he was alive," said the pilot. "Now the bugger's still flying around for free."

—Letter to Nick Berwian, August 31, 2003

I had nine wwoofers that summer. Two couples hiked in with me when I returned home after Max's porcupine encounter. One of these was from Calgary, the other comprised a Scottish man and an Australian woman. When various clients arrived, Swiss, German and Chinese-Canadian, it made for an interesting variety of accents about the place.

Three of the wwoofers were very hard workers; the fourth generally had something to complain about and of course gave the least input. Between them, however, they put a big dent in the trail work I had planned, and they were also a great deal of fun. I always give the wwoofers a chance to make bread if they wish, and this crowd got quite heavily into the culinary scene. For our final meal we had a spotted-dick-making competition accompanied by every kind of innuendo imaginable. The details would sound merely gross written out, but we all thought our jokes very funny at the time.

The second batch of wwoofers, who came during the last half of August, were a little more difficult to deal with. I was outside yet again for the second week of that month, speaking at the Sunshine Coast Festival of the Written Arts in Sechelt, and two wwoofers flew back home with me; the other three arrived a couple of days later on spare seats on client planes. This lot consisted of two Canadians (who had not met each other before), a New Zealand woman, a German and an Austrian. The Canadian man and the Austrian could already use chainsaws so they were very useful. The New Zealand woman was absolutely marvellous at everything she tackled. But unlike the first batch of wwoofers, these people did not gel as a group. Each one wanted to pull in a different direction. Accommodation was tight—Cabin One was available to them for some of the time, but when I needed it for paying guests, the wwoofers had to crowd into tents. Feeding them also created problems. Two of the wwoofers were vegetarians and the others were meat eaters, which would not have been difficult by itself, but one man who ate meat was allergic to nuts and fish and one of the vegetarians could not eat anything spicy. Sometimes I ended up cooking several separate meals. Five disparate strangers at once was obviously too many, especially when I had other visitors as well; on the other hand, I prefer to have more than one wwoofer at once as they are company for each other and less of a drain on my emotional resources.

The low-snow winter was the precursor of a hot, dry summer. Fires started burning all over British Columbia, those in the major centres making such momentous international news that Rosemary began to receive all kinds of concerned emails for me, from friends as far afield as Australia. Two large fires burned on the Chilcotin: one spanned the highway for more than 5 kilometres and the other, the Chilko Lake fire, eventually covered several thousand hectares and created huge quantities of smoke. But Nuk Tessli was situated upwind of these disasters. The air above my lake remained clear and sunny, and the views were rarely compromised. Because I can receive radio signals only in the dark hours, I rarely hear the news in summer and found it hard to believe visitors' tales of the destruction of forests and homes. I did lose a couple of clients: one was driving from Edmonton and decided to turn back at the British Columbia border (there was a very bad fire there, too); the other decided to stay in the States. Neither would have been here long, nor were they confirmed bookings, so I shrugged off the minor loss of income as just one of those things.

In August it rained a little and then stayed cool and damp, so fire was no longer a danger here, although the drought continued farther south and some of the biggest residential destruction in Kelowna and Barriere took place then. All that the wwoofers and my clients had to complain about, however, was the rain.

Toward the end of August, the Berkés, a French couple and their ten-year-old daughter arrived for a few days. They had found out about Nuk Tessli through the internet and were my first clients to book through that source alone: almost everyone else has come because they had read my books, heard the letters I wrote to Peter Gzowski's *Morningside* on CBC Radio, or had seen one of my slide shows. The Berkés were avid hikers. At the same time, a single Canadian man travelling with his dog rented a cabin for part of his stay. He also intended to spend time backpacking. I had all five wwoofers at that point but some of them also wanted to do camping trips, so by rotating the parties it was possible to keep everyone occupied and out of each other's hair.

The French family and the single man (and dog) decided to share a Beaver back to Nimpo Lake; there would be two spare seats on that plane, and two of the wwoofers chose to leave then, too. The plane was due around 10:00 a.m., but two hours later it still had not arrived. The weather was poor, and under those circumstances priority is given to people who absolutely have to be out in time for scheduled flights. I assumed that this was the reason for the delay. The westerly wind ceased and puffs of air started to come from the east, accompanied by a very black-looking sky toward Nimpo: it was obvious that the weather was deteriorating fast. Stewarts don't use the local radiophone frequency so I tried calling out on the long-distance channel to find out what was happening, but could not get through.

It is rare to have fog here, but at lunchtime the clouds suddenly rolled down to lake level. Moments later, to my immense surprise, a Beaver slipped over the ridge between my place and Avalanche Lake and skidded onto the water. "I can't believe you got in," I said to Ian, the pilot, as I met him on the wharf. "It's socked right down."

"Oh, it's still open at the other end of the lake," Ian said cheerfully. "I could see perfectly well as I touched down."

The French family, the man and his dog, and the two wwoofers climbed aboard. One of the wwoofers was like me—she had a flying phobia. "It's only twenty minutes," I told her, trying to make it easier for her. (I tell myself that every time, too.)

The plane swung out into the calm water. Aircraft lift off more easily if they head into the wind, even if the breeze is almost non-existent, and on this occasion the pilot had to taxi down to the far end of the lake first. As the sound of the motor chugged away, those of us left behind breathed a sigh of relief. Plane delays are always a nuisance: the clients get restless and no one can do anything or go anywhere because everything is packed. The situation had been exacerbated by the rain—everyone had to wait inside—but now we could relax a bit.

But when the plane reached the far end of my lake, there was none of the expected racketing roar that normally accompanies takeoff. Instead, the same chugging taxiing sound grew louder and louder until the plane was once more at my dock.

"I guess it wasn't open there any more," Ian grinned as he tied his plane onto the cleats.

The passengers disembarked. For some reason everyone, including the wwoofers, decided to come into my cabin. That made eleven of us (plus a dog) in a room that was crowded when three people made themselves at home in it. I made black tea, herb tea and coffee, and did what I always do when planes are overdue—got out the games box. For a couple of hours, the clients, the pilot and the two wwoofers who were hoping to leave amused themselves with Chinese puzzles and card games. Although it was raining heavily by this time, the other wwoofers decided they wanted a bit of space and they loaded a chainsaw and tools into a canoe and went up to the head of my lake to tackle the next job on the "do" list, which was to make some improvements to the portage. By around four in the afternoon, the dense cloud had lifted perhaps 50 metres above the lake and it looked a little brighter toward The Trench. It was still pretty black in the Nimpo direction, but Ian figured that if he could take off, he might be able to take his passengers out the long way around, via The Trench and Hunlen Falls. Everyone piled aboard

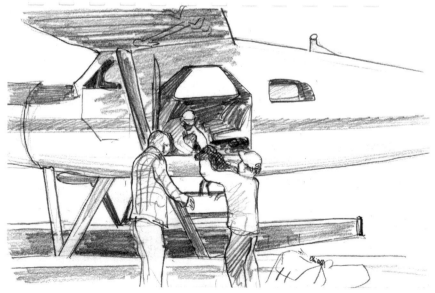

Loading the Beaver

again (the dog hated it as much as the phobic wwoofer and was shaking even harder); the plane chugged slowly to the far end of the lake and, with a bellowing roar, heaved itself into the air and skimmed the treetops above the cabin. Ian must have thought that the Avalanche Lake route looked all right, for he continued in that direction and the sound of the motor grew distant. But before it had gone completely, I heard it coming back again. My heart sank, but the plane stayed high and disappeared toward The Trench. The sound vanished completely this time and I trudged up the trail to the cabin, looking forward to an hour or so of blessed aloneness before the remaining wwoofers turned up for supper.

The peacefulness lasted all of five minutes. To my utter chagrin, the drone of the motor grew louder again. Soon the plane was hissing onto the rain-beaten lake and taxiing to the wharf. Ian told me he could have landed on either Avalanche Lake or Lonesome Lake but could not get any farther and figured everyone would be much more comfortable at my place. The poor phobic wwoofer. Until she stepped onto my dock, she had no idea that she was not at Nimpo. Even when they had flown low over the portage where the other wwoofers were working, she still hadn't cottoned on. She had merely thought, "That's funny. They've got a portage at Nimpo just like Chris's."

This time no one was interested in the games. Two more hours went by. Should I prepare a meal, or would they suddenly be able to depart when I had a great pile of food half-cooked? In the end I made a soup—or rather two soups, one vegetarian and one with meat. I had baked bread the day before, expecting it to last for a while longer, but it would all get eaten now. Ian looked at his watch. "If we don't get away before eight o'clock I guess we're stuck here," he said. When the magic hour came, everyone's gear was unloaded. Many pilots carry a sleeping bag as a matter of course, but Ian didn't. In twenty years of flying he had never before been stranded overnight. I had enough spare bedding to kit him out. Having so many guests at the same time had worked before because some of them had been out backpacking. But now they would have to crowd together in the cabins: it would have been miserable trying to put up a tent in that rain. Fortunately all the clients were treating it as an adventure (although I am not sure what the dog, who spent most of her time cowering in a corner of my cabin, was making of it all).

It was still socked in the following morning, but there was just the smallest breeze from the west, which was a very good indication that the fog would clear. I managed to get through to Stewarts on the radiophone. (The aircraft's radiophone doesn't work until the plane is in the air.)

"What's it like at Nimpo?" asked the pilot.

"Terrible," came the reply. Duncan Stewart's voice was the one that came over the phone and I could imagine him sitting at his desk in the lodge. "It's dumping rain and there is no sign at all of the mountains in your direction."

"The wind's changing and it's starting to clear from the west here," said Ian.

"Do you think you can get into Fish Lake?" Duncan asked.

We looked over toward the gap on Louise O'Murphy's left, and it did indeed look as though it might be possible to sneak in there, particularly as the cloud was now lifting by the minute.

"There's a party of three stranded there," Duncan continued. "We took them in yesterday morning for a day's fishing but couldn't get back in there to pick them up. They're experienced in the bush so I am sure they're okay, but they were not expecting to spend the night and the only shelter they have is the tarp we keep up there for emergencies. If you can get up there, pick them up and take them to Chris's. At least they can warm up a bit there."

So Ian went off and I put on the coffee pot. It takes me five or six hours to hike to Fish Lake but it is only minutes away by plane. When the wind is right I can hear aircraft taking off from there. But when the Beaver had climbed back into the air after picking up the stranded fishermen, its sound disappeared. The clouds were clearing rapidly, and Ian must have found a way back to Nimpo. My own clients were picked up a couple of hours later.

The most entertaining visitors of that summer came at the end of July. They were a freelance writer and a photographer contracted to *British Columbia Magazine* who were going to spend five days accumulating material for a full feature article slated to be published the following year. (It eventually came out in the fall of 2004 under the title "A Queendom of One.") This was good news indeed, for the magazine has a wide international distribution.

Rosemary and Dave Neads were going to visit at the same time. Ever mindful of the difficulty I have in getting fresh produce, Rosemary had not only brought vegetables from her garden, but also organized a delivery of two flats of apricots. Real fresh food is a great luxury at Spinster Lake. The stores around the float-plane base are stocked by outfitters from Edmonton—everything is packaged, canned or frozen, or it has travelled from California to Edmonton and back to the Chilcotin in refrigerated trucks. So Okanagan fruit was welcomed with open arms. I had no fridge, and the weather was hot, so they would have to be canned at once. While the photographer snapped pictures and the writer asked questions, I sweated over the roaring stove.

The writer and the photographer were assigned to Cabin One. The photographer elected to be downstairs—the windows there had better views and he did not want to miss a photo op if the light was right. The writer braved the steep ladder into the attic and spread his sleeping bag on a foamy on the floor up there. The following day we hiked up to the North Ridge. Both dogs had packs on, not because there was very much for them to carry but just to look good for the pictures. Patrice Halley, the photographer, loved dogs and spent a great deal of time and cookies trying to get them to pose the way he wanted, most often without success.

It usually takes somewhere between two and four hours to reach the treeline, depending on the fitness of the hikers and what they are interested in. Some like to gallop ahead and climb everything in sight; others prefer to examine every plant or photograph from every view. Our progress that day was very much a stop-and-start affair. Patrice had two backpacks full of equipment; he carried one in the normal manner and the other back to front so it hung across his chest. He was a man with tremendous energy. He would rush ahead, set up a photo op, stay put while we trudged past, then pick up all his stuff and run ahead of us again. It was exhausting just to watch him. Then he would see a flower he liked and we would have to wait twenty minutes while he set up the shot and tried to will the wind to stop blowing.

The weather was fabulous. The Chilko fire was raging somewhere to the east but there was no sign of it up on the North Ridge. The sky was blue and the mountains softened by only the faintest of summer hazes. Two days before I had indulged myself in a day alone among the flower meadows to do my own photography. That time of year is usually the peak of the season for the most colourful wildflowers, and I had not been disappointed. The meadows had been a little on the dry side but were ablaze with red paintbrush, yellow arnica, purple fleabane, white valerian and blue lupine. I looked forward to having my beautiful backyard spread all over the magazine's pages, but the two intervening scorching days had been enough to make the turning point, and the flowers had fried. In a wetter year the meadows would be spectacular for at least a further two weeks; I could not believe how quickly they had finished.

The writer, the older of the two journalists, was not able to accompany us all the way up to the ridge. He put it down to lack of sleep and told us that the mice had been very noisy in the ceiling above his head all night. But he said that as long as they *stayed* up there he would manage fine.

During his second night in the attic, however, he had been woken by a "mouse" running over his face. "It was yea big," he said, holding his hands about 20 centimetres apart, "and it had a furry tail."

That was no mouse—it must have been a packrat. No wonder he had complained of the noise. Those critters do get into that cabin sometimes, but the first lot of wwoofers had only just left, and the one who was most vociferous with her complaints had slept in the attic. She would surely have mentioned the animals if they had been around. I did not design the roof of the cabin well enough to keep small animals out; the only solution would be to set a trap. Was the writer prepared to deal with that, or should I wait until after he had gone? The other alternative was for him to sleep in a tent on one of the islands.

The writer chose to use the tent for the rest of his stay, and he never even mentioned the packrats in the article, which I thought was pretty decent of him.

Packrat

CHAPTER 11

Huckleberry Hound

Dear Nick,

The lake is grey and flecked with whitecaps, the murky sky has obliterated the mountains and rain spatters against the Monarch window. We've had intermittently squally weather since the end of August, nothing very bad and with some fairly pleasant hours in between, but it has been quite windy most of the time. Neither good spells nor bad spells have lasted very long. Which made yesterday a bonus, as I needed a calm day to go to Octopus Lake and return the trapper's canoe. I borrowed it at the beginning of summer when the bridge was underwater during the short, high runoff we had . . .

—Letter to Nick Berwian, September 18, 2003

The task had been on my "do" list for some time, but I had been waiting for a suitable day. It was often calm in the pre-dawn, when the stars shimmered in a velvet sky and their reflections streaked the still, black water, but by sunrise the wind had always started and clouds were racing from the west. Fighting to get a canoe up my own lake would have been bad enough, but at Octopus Lake the wind would have had an extra hour to increase its strength, and paddling against it would be a nightmare. One morning in mid-September, however, the dawn clouds moved slowly from the north and a hard frost crisped the boggy meadows, so I figured I might have a window of calm. I set off at sunrise and was soon hiking up the first part of the trail in icy blue shade. The fall colours were at their best: the huckleberry leaves' ruby red mixed with the softer reds and bronzes of the mountain rhododendron. By the time I reached the plateau at the top of the South Ridge, a thin skin of cloud had hazed the sun and the day remained quite chill. I was cold all the time and wished I had brought an extra sweater with me. The advantage of this coolness was that there was not a blackfly in sight: blackflies can be quite the pests once the heavier frosts start.

The trapper's canoe was just upriver from the bridge. When I reached it, a puff or two of wind blew into my face and I thought I might already be too late, but these died down and I was treated to a magical day. Octopus Lake is very shallow; the name aptly describes its marvellously contorted shoreline. I drifted slowly along while Monarch, Wilderness and Flat-top Mountains, newly brushed with snow, continuously rearranged themselves over their reflections. The rocks at their feet were accented by wind-tortured subalpine fir and the blazing scarlet of dwarf birch. The slow-moving air meant that a slab of high cloud persistently blocked the sun, but there was blue sky around its edges and the light had a marvellous pearly quality. The colour of the shaded landforms, the dark water streaked with occasional silver cat's-paws and the blood-coloured birch were very dramatic. I took several photos but feared the strong contrast would not be well recorded by the camera's implacable eye.

As soon as the people pressure eased off in September, there were berries to harvest. Of the several edible wild fruits in my neighbourhood, only two grow in sufficient numbers to make a picking expedition worthwhile. One is the crowberry, gathered by the First Nations people because of its quantity but not a gourmet's dream—it is very seedy and not flavourful. The bears love it, though, and their droppings are purple and full of seeds at this time of year. The other fruit is the black huckleberry. The bush on which it grows is the predominant understory vegetation of the drier areas of the forest, although unless there is a bit of underground water, such as in a gully, the plant may not have enough resources to produce fruit. At its tallest it can reach my waist, but it often sprawls on the ground; most plants reach a height somewhere in between.

The berry may be blue or a dark, purplish black, round or pear-shaped, and in good years, when the sun and rain fall just right, the fruits may be almost as large as commercial blueberries (to which they are closely related). They are not only common, but also delicious. In the spring, the plants are always laden with greenish little urn-shaped bells just as their leaves unfurl, but in the kind of dry summer we had just experienced, if they yield any fruit at all it is usually small and sparse. But when the remaining wwoofer, New Zealand Chris, and I set out with our pails early one September morning, we found that for some inexplicable reason, the crop was

Huckleberry

abundant. We would pick for a couple of days and then I would go on a canning binge, and by the end of the picking season I had put up thirty-two quart jars. I use the pressure canning method for most foods, but the huckleberries do not seal properly; for them the water-bath method works best. As I have limited stove-top space and my largest pot is the pressure canner, I can process only four jars at once, but by keeping spare jars and the berry pot hot, I can do several consecutive loads. If I have no guests, I do this operation in Cabin Two and keep the heat from the daylong roaring stove out of my living area.

Berry picker's backache can be a bit of a problem, but on the whole I like the picking season. I love to roam around my favourite spots and enjoy the sunlight filtering through the yellowing fall leaves. Migrating birds come through, also attracted by the fruit. Blackflies can be a real nuisance at that time, and I start picking early in the day in order to have a few hours free of them. On one occasion I noticed that the first patch of berries were all dusted with a white powder that at first I took to be some kind of mould. But it was a bloom of frost.

Bucky turned out to be a real huckleberry hound. All my dogs have nibbled at the berries once in a while, but Bucky scarfed them down like they were going out of style. His poop began to look just like a bear's. It wasn't long before I realized that he always found the best berries. I would start on a patch and listen for the slobbery chomping, and sure enough, the dog would have homed in on the most luscious fruit. I found out later that in some wine-growing areas in Europe, dogs are used to determine when the grapes are ripe. I wondered if I could hire Bucky out to the vineyards in the Okanagan.

New Zealand Chris was a prodigious worker. During her last days at Nuk Tessli she built rock steps, split an enormous stack of firewood and helped me haul the boards from a lumber-making area near the head of the lake, on a high knoll in a patch of beetle-killed pines some distance back from the water. All the wwoofers had been involved in the tedious chore of slicing off the boards, with which I planned to build a new deck area, a couple of benches and a structure to house a compost toilet. Hauling stuff home by canoe can be done only when the weather is calm. Most mornings it was possible to manage at least one load before the wind became too strong. The last one we fetched in falling snow, as the flakes spun to meet their black reflections on the slick surface of the water.

It was only after Chris had left Nuk Tessli that the weather really improved. I celebrated it and my remaining two weeks of solitude before embarking on the fall book tour by taking a hike up to the North Ridge. The nasal yank yank of a nuthatch was heard along Edith Creek and the Clark's nutcrackers were their usual noisy selves, but otherwise there was not a lot of avian activity, for the berries were finished. Higher, fresh moose prints were sharply impressed into the dusty trail above Wiggly Creek Meadow; superimposed upon them were the soft, sock-like tracks of a bear. In a dried pond, the bear's pawmarks were perfectly drawn, the toes clawless, the prints small— evidently a black bear. The dogs showed only cursory interest, so the animal was not within smelling distance.

Above the treeline the tundra was bleached with frost; all was pale: eggshell rocks in frost-white grasses. The flower meadows were painted burnt umber. In them, fluffy fleabane seedheads balanced above their wrinkled brown leaves. The arctic willow was gold where the wind had not destroyed it, and the sky blue upon blue upon blue.

From the North Ridge

In the lee of the saddle below Avalanche Lake Lookout, there were squiggles of new snow left after the last storm; these were the beginnings of next year's corniced drifts. The dogs at once flopped down and pressed their bellies against them, for it was windless and hot. A few pieces of old snow still lingered on the north side of the ridge, but they were barely distinguishable from the rocks, for the years of drought and shrinking had concentrated a millennium's worth of dust on their surface.

I walked slowly along the ridge, absorbing this bubble in time and space. Tiny scraps of red-gold snow willows winked amongst purple-black lichen. The summits along the ridge were thrones for the gods. Numberless, nameless peaks in old-summer nakedness spread like a wrinkled map. Waddington and entourage, 80 kilometres south, were hard-edged and white, like teeth on the curve of the world.

I dropped to the upper of the two tarns below the ridge and ate a lunch, washing it down with icy mountain water. No matter how dry the country is, it always stays full, even when the lower one is a puddle in the centre of a wide ring of silt-blackened rocks. It had been a day for fly hatchings. Earlier, I'd seen five loose-winged caddis adults mobbing a female, all tightly blundering on a small subalpine fir. Here, some species of fly with a centimetre-long orange body was barging around. These insects were not good fliers and often struck against my face. Countless numbers had landed in the tarn, some on their backs, their wings waterlogged and their legs uselessly waving. Those that had landed belly down swam infinitely slowly, paddling endlessly with their legs; then tiny puffs of wind would catch the sails of their wings and push them far off course. I fished one of them out of the water and placed it on a rock, thinking to rescue it from its watery grave, and noticed that it had two much smaller flies clinging to it. Were they a separate species or merely a different gender? Hundreds of these were also struggling all over the surface of the tarn. Once on the rock, the fly I had fished out never missed a beat. Its churning legs moved with the same laboured rhythm as in the water, but now they carried the fly and its cargo slowly over the rock's surface. When the rock ended, the insect entered the water as if it had never left, drawing slowly away from the shore and continuing its futile swim. What blind instinct is moving these creatures?

On another perfect late September day, I hiked to a waterfall. It is a drop of no great magnitude, but it tumbles down in a series of very pretty curtains linked by crystal pools. Wet-loving saxifrages cling to the rock cracks beside the water chutes, and above it is yet another lake in a cirque backed by a small, old, tired-looking glacier.

I had not gone that way for some years. To reach it, I walked to the far end of North Pass Lake and up Incompetence Creek (named by the trapping family: they were guiding hunters along there and when they came across twelve ptarmigan the hunters blasted off at them but never hit one). Being glacier fed, Incompetence Creek always has a good supply of water in it, even at this time of year. It takes me two or three hours to reach it from the cabin, so I am always ready for a lunch when I get there.

Having raised my head after drinking my fill, I was very startled to see a hand waving at me from the water. With nothing but rocks and tundra in the vicinity, size is not always easy to determine, and the hand looked very human.

It belonged, however, to a marmot that had died and become

wedged under the water among some rocks. It lay on its back and one of its forepaws stuck up into the air. The fur had rotted off the skin, which was now smooth and hairless, and the fingers were spread to their fullest. The tumbling swirl of the water waved the limb back and forth.

CHAPTER 12

The Helicopter Ride

Happy Christmas, Chris, and may warm winds blow over your lake all winter.

—Christmas card, December 2003

Dear Nick,

It is day three of a bad storm. I think about 20 centimetres of snow has fallen; it is very difficult to tell when it is blown about so much. The deck facing Monarch has remained completely clear, but there are major drifts in the lee of the cabin, and these have blocked my trails to the outhouse and the waterhole. Today, at sunrise, there were a few blue patches in the east and I was hoping for an improvement but they disappeared and the wind has grown even stronger. Trees thrash and scream and the building trembles and moans.

Walls of blowing snow obliterate the mountains and turn the far shore of the lake and the islands to vague lumps of grey. It seems to me there are bigger flakes mixed with this, so I think it is snowing from the sky as well. It is above freezing—the first time for a while—and the snow is sticking to the sides of trees and walls and windows. Where it is not clogging on the glass, it is running down like rain. At the porch end of the cabin it is eddying round: it was for conditions such as this that I built the porch. If it was not there, the snow would be covering everything: stacked wood, tools, dog kennels and dogs.

—Letter to Nick Berwian, March 8, 2004

Warm winds are the last thing I want during a Nuk Tessli winter. Unless it is cold enough to make good, solid ice I cannot go home, and once there, if the snow is not dry foot travel of any kind is difficult and I am frustratingly confined to a very limited area around the cabin. A mild winter used to bring more snow, but we don't even have that consolation any more. Last year there was barely 15 centimetres on the ground when I arrived right after Christmas. Some of this then melted in the big thaw, and only another 40 centimetres fell during the rest of that season. When I first came to Nuk Tessli, I considered a metre of pack to be a low-snow year but we have not had even that much for some considerable time.

I knew from both the radio and reports gleaned from the Chilcotin that the fall of 2003 had been even milder than the year before. There was no point, therefore, in rushing back to Nimpo, so I spent Christmas down at the Coast with friends and drove north on the 27th and 28th of December. The ice at Nimpo was actually not too bad, but then an even more serious problem reared its ugly head. There were no pilots available, or at least none that were prepared to fly me home. Nimpo Lake used to be a haven for ski-plane enthusiasts, but now they've all melted away like ice in a thaw. One of the people who used to do a lot of flying for me no longer lives in the area. A plane that had flown me in on other occasions had been crashed by friends of the owner and destroyed. Floyd, my usual standby, who had never before spent a winter away from Nimpo, was visiting down in the States and it was not known when he would return.

Another pilot who might have obliged had a skis-only rig. Planes with a hydraulic wheel-ski combination, such as Floyd's, could take off from the Anahim airport runway when the lake conditions were poor and pump the skis underneath when the plane was in the air. But a skis-only rig could not be used until the snow had sufficient depth, and right now, the snow was so low at Anahim that grass was sticking through it on the strip.

This was devastating news. The thought of having to spend a lengthy period of time at the Nimpo cabin was horrifying. Mary has always been a great landlady, but I've never liked staying there. The cabin's saving graces are that it is convenient and dirt cheap, and Mary is a good and welcoming friend. The building itself is a wreck—it was erected on a bog into which it is relentlessly sinking; because of the bog it is impossible to jack the cabin up and put foundations underneath it, and it was not constructed well enough to move. It cannot be heated in cold weather or cooled in hot weather; there is no handy water supply, and in winter it is shaded by trees and no sun reaches it until almost noon. The bog heaves mightily when the frost goes out of the ground and the constantly shifting joints let in mosquitoes and mice—no amount of blocking can prevent them. To add to the discomfort, the area around it is far too crowded. I simply dislike living with other people breathing down my neck. In summer tourists stay at the resort, and in winter snowmobiles whine on the lake and yard lights ruin the night sky. To be there for a day or two while passing through was no hardship: the thought of having to live there for the next three months until the spring book tour took me away again was appalling.

I widened my search for a suitable aircraft, phoning people I barely knew and even complete strangers as far afield as Williams Lake. One person who owned a resort some distance north of Nimpo said he would be able to fly me home later in the winter, probably at the end of January, but the price he quoted was very high. The only other aircraft available were helicopters. A small one used to be based north of Anahim—it had transported me into Lonesome Lake when I house-sat for John Edwards after his brother had died. But that craft was no longer in the area, and the other two outfits were widely spaced, one near Tatla Lake in the east and the other in the Bella Coola Valley. A four-seater helicopter charged around $1,000 an hour; a larger one was correspondingly more expensive, and the trip from either place to my lake and back would probably take an hour at least. So there it was. Either I waited for a month for the plane, which would not be inexpensive, or I went home sooner by helicopter.

When a plane was available, the organization of my freight was not so crucial. I could expect another flight for one reason or another in the middle of winter and ask for mail and any necessary supplies to be sent in then. I certainly would not be able to afford a second helicopter flight, so everything I could conceivably need would have to go in with me. If I had known of this situation the summer before, I would have stockpiled dog food and other heavy stuff but of course had not budgeted for this event.

White Saddle Helicopters in the east quoted me a lower price, but the aircraft the proprietor had at that time was smaller (he has a bigger one now) and my dogs and myself would take up half the freight allowance. I did not think I could get the rest of what I needed in it. That left West Coast Helicopters, based at the Bella Coola Valley airport. Even that was not going to take place instantly because the pilot, Richard Lapointe, was not going to be at work until January 9. He would give me a very good rate—$1,600 including taxes. Dave and Rosemary Neads were planning a trip to Costa Rica that February. It was going to cost them less to get there than it would cost for me to go home.

I would have to drive to the helicopter base and leave my truck there, otherwise I would be charged for the extra half-hour flight time for the aircraft to reach Nimpo Lake. Richard wanted to leave around 10:30 a.m. to give himself plenty of leeway during the short day. From Mary's resort to the Bella Coola Airport is more than two hours' drive under the best of conditions. Because of their diverse altitudes and relationship to the Coast Range (the one is high on the dry eastern side, the other at sea level on the wet west coast), the climate of the two places is vastly different. The road between them runs through the Tweedsmuir Provincial Park and the country is wild and uninhabited. What conditions would be like on The Hill, the 30 kilometres of switchbacks that links the Chilcotin with the Bella Coola Valley, must always be guesswork in winter.

There had been no great amount of snow anywhere, so that probably would not be a problem, but the temperatures were usually well below freezing on top and often above freezing at the bottom. To a greater or lesser degree, therefore, ice could be expected somewhere along the way; as some of the hairpin bends reach a grade of 18 percent, I figured I would have to allow extra time in case I ran into problems. Add to that the fact that I would need to load the last of my freight into the truck (the produce was in Mary's root cellar and the meat was in her freezer), and I figured I should prepare to leave at 7:00 a.m.

Before loading the perishables I phoned Richard to see what the weather was doing down below. Conditions had not been all that stable, and even though the sky was clear at Nimpo, it could easily be pouring with rain down there. But Richard said it was looking good. It was apparently above freezing at the airport; Mary's yard thermometer read –10°C.

So I loaded the truck, scraped what ice had not yet melted off the windshield, and set off. It had been quite dark at seven, but as I drove west, light came into the sky. At the top of The Hill I was treated to a spectacular panoramic sunrise of vivid pink icefields and clouds all tumbled together above the great yawning pit of the Bella Coola Valley.

The valley is narrow, some 80 kilometres long between The Hill and the salt chuck, and rarely more than a kilometre wide. Its glacier-scraped sides are often sheer. The road down the cliff was packed snow, well sanded and with good traction all the way to the bottom. Halfway down the mountains a skin of cloud was spread like a tablecloth from side to side of the valley; above it soared rugged rocky peaks to 2,500 metres in height. I wondered about the cloud cover, but it was thin and gauzy, and having passed through it I could see bits of blue sky showing through. When the hard-top starts at the bottom of The Hill, there is always a risk of black ice so I drove with care, but it was soon evident that things were thawing even in the upper part of the valley. Remnants of dirty old snow lay beside the road but the ground was largely bare. Everything dripped.

At the airport (where the temperature was now 5°C), a large, smart, dark grey helicopter with blue and green trim stood in front of a hangar. It was an A-star. I had not met the pilot before but he knew my area because he had flown in the logs for Mary's Wilderness Lake cabin. Richard is a small man, not only short but thin to the point of emaciation; one might almost wonder about his health were it not for his boundless enthusiasm for life in general and his helicopter in particular. The helicopter is used for every conceivable purpose, including medical emergencies, but Richard and his friend also run a heli-skiing business. Two ski-length metal baskets were attached to the sides of the aircraft; they were ideal to carry my meat, the front quarter of buffalo that had been cut into four lumps. This would not only keep the meat cool but also separate it from the dogs.

There was plenty of space in the chopper's cab; it was a great change from the way I usually fly, either elbow to elbow with freight or with a monster dog on my lap. The flying phobia is always there, however, and it never fails to spoil the best of flights. The motor fired up for a few minutes, and with no change at all in the beat of the rotors we slowly and steadily lifted off the ground. It was remarkably quiet. I was sitting in the back with the dogs to make sure they behaved themselves and was wearing a headset so that I could converse with the pilot, but even without the headset it would almost have been possible to have a normal conversation. The A-star is a luxury craft indeed.

We began to drift up-valley over winter-brown cottonwoods that lined the black river with its dirty white old-snow banks. We were only just over treetop level and seemed to be moving very

slowly, but our forward speed was 190 kilometres per hour, about the same velocity at which a Cessna 185 travels. And yet the sensation of movement was very gentle, even though we were coasting along much closer to the ground than a plane would normally do.

I had assumed that we would fly back up the Bella Coola Valley to the bottom of The Hill, follow the Atnarko River up The Trench and over Lonesome Lake, then hop into my lake via the low pass I can see from the cabins. That was the way I had travelled on foot when I had first visited Nuk Tessli and most certainly would have been the route the pilot of a plane would choose. To my amazement, however, we steered straight to the valley's precipitous wall, nudged up into a gap I was not even aware of, then wove a course right through the middle of the mountains. We broke through the flimsy cloud and entered a magical land of brilliant sun, utramarine shadows, black rock, turquoise crevasses and white snow. Because they are so close to the sea, these mountains can receive a huge snowfall, and this keeps the treeline at a very low elevation. When we reached the same altitude as my lake, which is 300 metres below the treeline, we had left all traces of vegetation far behind. There wasn't very much snow this year, though; the mountain's bones were showing through like the ribs on a hungry dog.

Up here it was windy. Snow plumes blew from the ridges, and as we breasted gaps through the main Coast Range, the chopper swayed gently from side to side—a very different feeling to the hard bangs that planes register when they hit pockets of turbulence. Richard explained that the choppers ride wind better because the rotors cut up the air. And still we slowly climbed, so gently, and so close to some of the ridges, that I felt I could step out onto them. Now we could see the bigger peaks: 3,200-metre Talchako Mountain and then my own guardian, Monarch Mountain, at nearly 4,000 metres. It looked quite slim and needle-like from this perspective, very different from the sprawling mass I see through my window. Behind it dozens of blue-slashed glaciers tumbled into the great Monarch Icefield. When people came to my place and raved about their spectacular flight-seeing tours I never believed I would ever experience them. A flying phobia puts the damper on that kind of thing. But not only was I now up here, I found I was actually enjoying it. It was a marvellous sensation—the first flight I have ever experienced that I did not want to end.

Then we were crossing The Trench, quite a bit farther south than where Lonesome Lake is situated, and through the gaps in the lower peaks in front of us was the great blue plateau of the Chilcotin. In the foreground lay the white Rorschach blot of my lake. We touched down on the ice in front of the cabins. Twenty minutes' flying time north was Nimpo Lake: I had driven for two and a half hours and had lost over a thousand metres of elevation, then had ridden for a further thirty-five minutes and gained 1,600 metres in height to get home.

I needed to mail some photographs that were stored in the cabin, and this was probably going to be my only chance to get mail out this winter, so I left Richard with the aircraft while I struggled up the steep, rocky trail. The snow was only knee-deep, but it had been cold at one point early in the season (and was still below freezing up here) with the consequence that the snow had the texture of ball bearings. This is the worst type of snow to break trail in because it

won't pack down. It was going to be a monstrous job hauling all that heavy freight up to the cabin through this; it would likely take me all of the remaining daylight hours. Where are my wwoofers when I really need them?

It was the work of a few minutes to dig out the photographs and package them, and I also took time to put a match to the stove, in which I had laid the fire before I left, and scoop up a large metal bowl of snow to start melting water. I would cut a waterhole in the lake in a day or two when all my other chores were done.

I stepped back outside to find that Richard had been busy. He had been unloading the freight, not directly onto the ice, but onto a big cargo net. He told me to restrain the dogs so that they would not run into the tail rotor, then fired his aircraft up again and took off. Up he went, and at the end of a long rope, the freight went with him. He cleared the trees that surround the cabin and dropped the freight right in front of my door. After he had landed, he even helped me carry the produce inside and heave the meat into the attic out of the reach of the dogs. Apart from a couple of boxes of documents that would be unpacked later, the whole of the freight was taken care of in about thirty minutes.

Is it any wonder that I am totally in love with helicopters?

How short the days are in January. Already the sun was low and the light long and golden. Richard took off and headed into the sunset, and I was on my own again for the winter. I would have to leave again in the middle of March to make final preparations for the spring book tour, but even allowing for the late arrival I could still look forward to more than two months of freedom. Winter is my creative time, and I could not wait to start work on the two manuscripts I had in progress and to do some printmaking. Then there was all that luscious reading to do. I never read well when I am travelling outside or have too many visitors at Nuk Tessli, and now I could look forward to a veritable orgy of books.

Very little more snow fell that winter. The maximum depth around the cabins was maybe 60 centimetres. Snow is far more important than rain to this environment. Rain runs down the steep mountainsides without doing a lot of good, but snow allows the water to seep gently into the soil all summer. It was a very stable winter, very little wind, and temperatures were never very cold. Some afternoons were hot enough that I could sit on the deck, but it usually froze at night and travelling around on skis, while never easy (shallow snow fails to cover all the bumps and hollows, and it is difficult to get around in the forest), was pleasant as long as I stuck to broken trails or the ice. Unbroken snow was hard work: because it was so shallow the skis sank through it and tangled with brush and rocks at every step.

One hazily sunny day about a month after I had been home, I had just returned from an outing when I heard a small aircraft approach. In other years there would often be private planes flying overhead in good weather, but this was the first aircraft I had heard this year. What's more, it was not coming from the Nimpo Lake direction, but from the south. Soon I could hear that it was not a plane but a helicopter. It buzzed low over the cabin and prepared to land. It was an A-star and was painted dark grey with blue and green trim.

Richard and two friends had been at a meeting on Vancouver Island and were returning to Bella Coola. The friends were wearing town shoes and a bit aghast at having to walk through the several centimetres of loose snow that lay on the ice, but they made it into the cabin. And they carried with them two boxes of fresh produce, bought that very morning at a grocery store in Courtenay. I was dumbfounded. Bananas, yogourt, liquid milk, avocados. What treats! I stock my larder with potatoes, cabbage, carrots, onions and turnips, and grow alfalfa, radish, sunflower and lentil sprouts for fresh greens, but these become tedious after a while. To have such exotics as bananas and avocados brought fresh to my door in the middle of winter was astounding.

I would love to have booked Richard for a flight back out again in March, but I simply did not have another $1,600. I made preparations to get out on foot. I had not done a marathon winter trip for many years. If I went down the river (mostly on frozen lakes)

I could reach one of the cabins belonging to Stewarts Lodge in a day. It was not a very comfortable cabin in winter—the only heat was generated by a wood cookstove with a microscopic firebox, but it was marginally better than making a camp in the snow. The second day on the trek would be the worst. No lakes to make life easy, and a rough hodgepodge of spruce swamp, windfalls and rocky hummocks. Once I got through that, I would be on the frozen Charlotte Lake, whose ice would probably still be good (it is the latest in the area to freeze and the earliest to go out), after which there would be logging roads, snowmobile trails and people.

The snow at Nuk Tessli had still not consolidated, so any unbroken country was going to be very hard work. Conditions would likely be different lower down, but I had no way of knowing whether they would be better or worse. The snow would probably be less deep, but it might be rotten or icy, and trying to manoeuvre skis or snowshoes over thousands of windfalls under those conditions would be exhausting and very slow going indeed. I no longer had the stamina of ten years ago and wondered if I would be able to manage the trip. Moreover, after nearly a decade, menopause had not lost its grip on me and the excessive sweating continuously soaked my clothes, making hypothermia a very real danger.

I spent a couple of days breaking trail halfway to the cabin on the lake the Stewarts have named Davidson, but the experience did nothing to make me think a winter hike to the road was going to be in any way enjoyable. Two weeks before I was due to leave, however, who should turn up but Floyd, with a package of mail and one of Mary's friends. Once again Floyd agreed to fly me out in time for the spring book tour.

CHAPTER 13

Nuk Tessli Goes High-Tech

How strange it is to be surrounded by endless untracked forest and receive distant, alien signals. These unseen waves, plucked from the firmament by tangled threads of wire, are nothing short of miraculous. Imagine the billions of invisible, inaudible messages batting back and forth around our globe, unrealized unless one has the means to trap them. The air is full of "a thousand jangling instruments" indeed—but only if one has a battery!

—Excerpt from *Gentian Violet*,
the thirty-times-rejected murder mystery

From: Chris Czajkowski
Date: Thursday, June 10, 2004, 8:46 a.m.
To: Rosemary Neads
Subject: It's a go!
      You have the unmitigated privilege of being the recipient of the first email ever from Nuk Tessli.
      Isn't this fun!!

C

I love to visit the prairies, that wide tawny landscape under the great open sky with its friendly, shabby little towns clustered around a railway station and the open lot where the wooden grain elevator used to be. During the spring of 2004, after I had toured the Okanagan and southern British Columbia,

I travelled through much of Alberta with my books and slides. But it is in the mountains where my heart lies. There is something about the awkward juxtaposition of their angles that paradoxically soothes my soul. Part of it, perhaps, is the knowledge that human endeavours are still subservient in this environment, although its protection is largely a question of economics. Today's technology can easily reduce the largest mountain to rubble if someone thinks they can make money by doing it.

The spring book tour was the least stressful I have ever taken. One major difference was that I had a little money in the bank before I even started it—most unusual. And in all those kilometres of road travel, nothing major went wrong with the truck (the year before, it blew a motor and the replacement took all my book tour profits). I did well enough through honoraria and book and art sales to know that I would be able to pay all my immediate bills. It was a heady feeling. And right then, just when the rest of my life was beginning to shape up, there was good news from a publisher. *Lonesome*, after two rejections and two further years of hollow promises, was accepted by Touchwood Editions, a division of Heritage House. The book was going to be released in the fall. And as if that wasn't enough to be thankful about, the upcoming summer's bookings for the Nuk Tessli Alpine Experience were double those of the previous year and by far the best I'd ever had—I was actually going to make some money from the eco-business for a change. The future was looking very good indeed.

The moment I returned to Nimpo Lake to start organizing things for my flight home, things started to go wrong.

The morning after I arrived, I took the dogs up the power line behind my cabin, well away from Mary's menagerie, and let Max off the lead. (I would never trust Bucky, but Max was more predictable in his activities and could thus have a limited amount of freedom.) Within minutes, he gave a yelp. He had made exactly that noise only once before in his life—when he had twisted something in his left hind leg. That time it had occurred on a book tour, on one of the few occasions he had been running loose; he was subsequently on the lead for most of the following month, and the leg seemed to cure itself. As soon as I got him home, however, every time he had a lot of exercise, particularly if he was swimming, he became very lame. At the end of the summer I took him to a vet who said the problem was a cruciate ligament and the operation would cost $800 with no guarantee of a cure. Max was still a young dog then, and although I could ill afford it, I went ahead with it and he recovered completely.

I knew at once that he had done the same thing, this time with the other hind leg. I phoned the vet in Williams Lake and was shocked to find that the operation was now going to cost $1,600 and there was still no assurance that it would work. Max was no longer young. This kind of expense would have me in the red again. He would recover reasonably well without the operation if he did not have a lot of heavy exercise, but unless I spent a great deal of money, his life at Spinster Lake was finished. The accident happened on the Friday before the May long weekend. It was not life-threatening, so I could not get a vet to examine him until the Tuesday. I managed to arrange an appointment for Tuesday afternoon, ostensibly to have him looked at, but by the time I loaded the truck for the four-hour drive to Williams Lake that morning, I had come to the terrible conclusion that I was going to have to have Max put down. I tried to get hold of the SPCA and the breeder—the only people whom I knew might help me save Max's life—but I had only their business numbers and would not be able to talk to them until I arrived in Williams Lake.

I have had to shoot two different dogs at Nuk Tessli, and I had thought that taking a dog to a vet for the job would be easier. But it was, if anything, worse. I was crying so hard on the drive into town I could barely see and several times wondered if I would get there in one piece.

The breeder, a dentist, could not take Max: she had three Akitas of her own who were very territorial and would not abide an intruder. But after my repeated pleas she agreed to see what she could do. An hour before execution time she told me to bring Max to the surgery: she would keep him tied outside the waiting room while she finished her day's work. It was raining and I chained Max to the railings of a small deck so that he could shelter under a tiny overhang. He seemed a bit bemused but not too unhappy. I knew it was unlikely that I would ever see him again.

A short while later I received a call. One of the dentist's clients had seen the dog, asked why he was tied there and at once decided to take him home. He had two dogs already but one, a poodle, was eighteen years old and on its last legs. Max would live at the edge of town; forest was to be his backyard. I was sorry to see him go, and I still miss him, but anything was better than having him destroyed.

But now I needed another large dog in a hurry. Two are a nuisance when I am travelling outside, but one is not enough for backpacking. I used to wear a 20-kilogram pack as if it were an overcoat, but my knees no longer tolerate a lot of weight and the dogs make a great deal of difference to my hiking range. With two of them, I can hike for three days without carrying much more than a sleeping bag and camera equipment. They carry their own food, my food, cooking equipment, spare clothes and the tent. For trips longer than three days I have to put some of the food in my pack—usually their kibble, which is lighter than my food (especially if I take along some homemade bread!).

The SPCA, when I finally managed to get hold of them, said, inevitably, "Oh you're just too late for a lovely large, friendly husky cross. We had him for weeks but he was taken two days ago. We don't have anything big enough for you otherwise." However, the lady said she had heard of a private outfit that dealt only with bigger dogs. Their home base was about an hour and a half's drive east out of Williams Lake (the opposite direction to Nimpo). I managed to reach them, and they offered to bring the dogs half the distance. I explained what I needed—no excessive barking, good with people, good size and preferably a good winter coat—and they brought with them a German shepherd cross Australian shepherd, a very funny-looking dog with a blotchy grey coat, and another Rottweiler cross, this one apparently with some bull mastiff in him. The shepherd was very gentle and apparently excellent with livestock, which would have been a bonus, but I was leery of potential hip problems, common in these breeds; also, he had not been neutered, which would have been more expense (this was a private outfit, so the cost was not included in the price). The other dog was young, tall, Rottweiler-coloured and full of beans, and he had been fixed. I asked the rescue people why he was so skinny. His ribs stood out like piano keys and his hip bones were sharp triangles above his powerful hams. His coat was dull and oily, and it stunk.

They said they had got him from the pound. He seemed, however, to be good-natured, and he and Bucky got on instantly—so well, in fact, that I could put them in the dog crate together right away. I handed over the $150 the rescue people asked for (they wanted cash, not a cheque), and it was only later that I looked at the papers they had given me. They indicated that the rescue people had been caring for this dog for six weeks. Why was he in such poor condition? With me, after a good worming and a few days' steady feeding, he looked a great deal better already. I later heard some suspicious stories about

Raffi

this rescue outfit and concluded that something fishy was going on. A few months down the road, the rescue outfit was apparently charged with several counts of cruelty.

They had certainly been right when they told me the dog had a good disposition, though. He was excellent with people and has proved to be more biddable than any of the other animals I have had, with the exception of my first dog Lonesome. I called him Raffi (short for giraffe) because of his extraordinary long neck and legs; he is a dog with a great capacity for enjoyment and bounds through life wearing a big, happy grin. (His only problem is that he thinks he is a lapdog, and if anyone sits down he tries to get at least the front half of his body aboard.)

The dog crisis was not the only setback I had while passing through Nimpo Lake. I also received a letter from my insurance broker. The Land Office demands that I have $1 million liability insurance before I operate on Crown land, and the insurance company I had been dealing with for ten years suddenly said they "do not handle" my kind of business. What they thought they were handling over the last decade I can't imagine. The broker told me that any other insurance company would require me to do a wilderness first-aid course before they would cover me. My outdated industrial first-aid certificate did not count.

Wilderness first-aid courses do not grow on trees. Williams Lake never offers them. I would have to go farther afield, to Prince George or Vancouver—but were even these places going to run them in time? My first visitors were due in three weeks. I was incensed that the insurance company had given me so little notice. They said they were legally obliged to inform me of things like this only thirty days beforehand; as I had been away, the letter had sat at Nimpo for half of that time.

That is when I learned that it is impossible to deal with insurance companies directly. One has to go through an agent. The agent in Williams Lake took a shrug-the-shoulders attitude. I tried other agents, explaining that mine was a comparatively risk-free business and that in fifteen years of operation I had never had a claim. But they would not step on each other's toes. The word "eco-tour" put the fear into them. They were, after all, city people who sat in an office and knew nothing outside their tiny circle of existence. They obviously equated my benign and gentle business with snowmobilers caught in avalanches, hunters shooting each other, extreme skiers and so on. Through Rosemary's search on the internet, I made contact with an offshore company that would charge me over $2,500, a 500 percent increase over what I had been paying, and I would also have to agree to a $5,000 deductible. Moreover, I had to come up with a waiver: I adapted a document from a mountain-guide organization that basically stated, in a thousand different ways, that I and my landlord (the BC government), and the Queen, were not liable for any injury even if it was our fault.

The government states in its agreement for my licence of occupation that without the million-dollar liability, I would have to close the business down. But I went home uninsured anyway. Even if a wilderness first-aid course had been available, I could not bear the idea of going back to Vancouver after having already been on the road so long. Just before the first visitors were due to arrive, the Williams Lake agent informed me that the original insurance company had relented and would continue to serve me this year, but I would have to take the wilderness first-aid course and find a new insurer before the next season.

I have told more than one interviewer, in my travels around the country, that I would rather have the internet than plumbing. Rosemary had been doing a marvellous job of organizing my business life for me, but it could never be the same as having direct contact with my customers, and internet access at Nuk Tessli had been on my wish list for a long time. With my laptop I could handle my own email through a telephone line whenever I was outside, but a satellite connection had hitherto seemed financially out of reach. The book tour had been satisfactory, however, and I was counting on the larger-than-usual number of booked summer tourists to bring in a bit of extra cash to play with. All this coincided with an introductory offer by a company called LinCsat (now Xplornet) that was slashing $500 off the price for the satellite modems and dish, and offering free installation, as long as it was paid for before the end of April. I had explored several other alternatives, and this seemed not only cheaper, but also something that would work at Nuk Tessli.

Having internet access at Spinster Lake was, I figured, really going to freak out the wilderness purists. Many people were horrified when I wrote about bringing a computer to Nuk Tessli twelve years ago. For them it totally spoiled the image they had of a life close to nature, despite the fact that I was very dependent on a very natural resource—the sun—to operate it. What made their attitude even more puzzling to me was the fact that high-tech items such as chainsaws and planes, which operate on polluting non-renewable fossil fuel, and toilet paper and axes and sleeping bags, which are made in smelly factories, were allowed, but computers were not. One woman even wrote a book review in a major newspaper to the effect that I was basically cheating and had pulled the wool over readers' eyes by calling myself a wilderness dweller and having a computer in the background. Interestingly, these kinds of critics are always cossetted by every convenience imaginable. Such comments merely show the supreme ignorance many people have about life in the backcountry. If she moved out here, would she, a person who makes her living by writing, expect to produce articles with a burnt stick on birchbark?

I knew very well that the prices quoted by Xplornet would be only a fraction of what I would have to spend. For instance, "free installation" referred to the Williams Lake area. Not only would I have to pay the technician's flights from Nimpo to Nuk Tessli, I would also have to fork out $320 for his eight-hour drive to the float-plane base and back. To keep the costs down as much as possible, I arranged for the technician to meet me at the Tweedsmuir Air dock on the day I wanted to fly home. The dogs, the equipment and ourselves would need the larger Beaver for the flight in, but the smaller plane would pick up the technician, and it would be loaded with the rest of my most urgent freight. I would have had to pay for one plane for myself in any case; by sharing with the installer I would need to charter only one extra flight instead of two.

The location of the satellite dish would be based on several criteria. It had to face the sun at 11:00 a.m. in summertime; it had to be mounted on something solid; there must be no trees in the way; it must not be installed under eaves where snow might crash onto it; it must not be placed where people might walk in front of it during transmission because the concentrated rays were known to be harmful. I had shown the technician some snaps of the place before he came, but he could not really judge the situation until he was on the ground. The gable ends of the cabin seemed to provide the best anchorage: I could see that the technician favoured the Monarch end of the building, but I worried about the fierce winds that can power up from the lake there and persuaded him that the porch gable end would be best. There was a small tree in the way; it could easily be removed, but it supported my radiophone aerial. So first we had to relocate that. I had a few poles for potential building projects lying near the cabin, and we placed the antenna on one of those and attached it to the woodshed. All the wiring had to be rerouted, and the technician crawled around, detaching it from under the bed and fitting everything neatly with his cordless drill. (Would I have enough power to run such a handy tool?)

Another extra expense was the purchase of a new (used) laptop. The first one I had bought was not powerful enough and could not be upgraded. A desktop would have been a lot cheaper, but Dave Neads, who runs a house full of electrical appliances including a satellite internet connection, recommended the laptop, as it would use less power. The technician had originally hoped to fly back out to Nimpo that same day, but he had arrived at the float-plane base later than he intended, and having to remove the radiophone aerial first delayed him further. He worked late into that evening programming my laptop and also fixing some other bits and pieces that were not working right. The special offer that the company had made was a good deal in the first place, but all the extra work that the technician did made it a real bargain.

Yet more expenses reared their ugly heads, however. I'd had the solar power system for about fourteen years, and had renewed the two 6-volt deep-cycle storage batteries about eight years previously, which was pretty much their life expectancy. The satellite modems, I discovered, used a great deal more power than the computer alone; that, plus some very black skies, reduced the life of the batteries even further. Soon they were incapable of storing a charge for very long, and the only time I could work was when the sun shone directly onto the panels. Replacing the batteries was going to be a problem. Because of the acid they contain, wet-cell batteries cannot be shipped by regular carrier. The nearest supplier was on the far side of Williams Lake.

However, friends were due to visit in early July; they were to fly from England to Vancouver, where they would rent a car to drive up to Nuk Tessli. They would be passing the solar-equipment supplier, and I wondered if they could pick up some new batteries en route.

I could now communicate with the Neadses by email almost as easily as chatting to them on the phone. I asked Dave about my solar panels. I had two small ones joined together on a frame that I could move about to catch every available gleam of sun when light was scarce in the winter. Last fall, however, a freak gust of wind had flipped them over, face down onto a rock. The glass surface of one of the panels had shattered into a million segments around a great bulging bruise. Dave said the broken one would still probably work to a certain degree, but he could get me a really good deal on a new one, and what I also needed was a gizmo for regulating the power both in and out of the batteries. A good meter cost $500, he said, but was well worth it for by monitoring the power flow I could extend the life of the batteries.

All this was beginning to sound rather complicated so I asked Dave and Rosemary if they would like to come in at the same time as my English friends: I would pay their share of the plane and we could have an enjoyable visit at the same time. I tried not to think about the mounting bills. I was, perforce, going to make all that money out of the tourist business; surely that would cover the extra expenses.

They flew in a week or so later and Dave spent all day rigging up my new system. It now looks very professional, with all the wires tidily coiled out of the way instead of the coloured spaghetti I set

Solar panels

up on my own. The broken panel was apparently still 60 percent effective—Dave had a gizmo to test that as well. The new panel was as large as the two old ones put together (and four times as efficient), which made the frame to which they were now attached too heavy to move around easily. This meant we needed a good permanent site as far away from tree shadows as possible, so a platform was built for them on the rocks by the lakeshore. Throughout my tenure in the wilderness I have always tried to blend my structures into the landscape as thoroughly as possible. The cabins have been built out of untreated logs—many already weathered—and the roofs are brown: people have told me that they have flown overhead without any idea that the cabins existed. The panels must be exposed to operate efficiently, which means that they can be seen from far up the lake. But if I want the miracle of the internet, I will have to accept that the panels and dish are now part of my landscape, too.

PART TWO

The Lonesome Lake Fire

CHAPTER 14

The Lightning Strike

Mazur [Steve Mazur, regional manager for environmental stewardship, Ministry of Water, Land and Air Protection] stated that on June 21st, 2004, BC Forest Service received a report that a small fire had started from a lightning strike deep within the [Tweedsmuir] park boundaries on the plateau east of Turner Lake.

After some initial attack work, BCFS reviewed the situation. Mazur explained that Forestry reported to Parks that they felt the area was too steep for the ground assault. They further felt that an air attack was not safe because of approach and turning clearances. Although the area was a "full suppression zone" according to their mandate, BC Parks agreed to allow the fire to burn.

—From an article by Rosemary Smart,
Coast Mountain News, August 5, 2004

From: *Rosemary Neads*
To: *Chris Czajkowski*
Sent: *Thursday, June 24, 2004, 9:15 a.m.*
Subject: *Smoke.*

Good morning Chris!

There were strikes both at Turner Lake and in the Klinaklini last night. You could be getting the smoke from either of them. The Turner Lake strike is supposed to be a small one but it doesn't look that tiny from here. The smoke is rolling right up the Hotnarko and into our valley. The smell is pretty strong . . .

Late May and June had been very hot and dry. The ice had gone out three weeks early at Nimpo and was likely to have done so at Spinster Lake, but what with the dog and insurance crises I didn't arrive home until June 7, and by then it was very difficult to judge when the last of the ice had left. (Compare this with the previous year, when I had been prevented from flying home until June 5.)

The water level of Spinster Lake was extremely low. In part, this was a result of normal breakup conditions. There is well over a metre's difference between high water and low water, and the level is at its highest when the ice goes out. Unless there is a lot of snow in the mountains, or there are very heavy spring rains, the lake drops rapidly within the first two or three weeks. Nonetheless, this year's level was alarming.

Part of the wharf is built on logs laid upon the shoreline rocks. These are anchored by long poles, whose lower ends are nailed into the logs with heavy spikes, and whose upper ends are strapped to trees along the bank. During a high runoff year, the fixed wharf floats: if a person steps on it, he might have to be careful that the water does not spill over the tops of his gumboots. Attached to the fixed wharf is a float. When I first arrive home in summer, the float deck is often higher than the fixed wharf. This year it was at least 15 centimetres lower. Close to the wharf is a little pocket garden. In a high-water year, even the top terrace may be covered with water. Most years, however, I can plant that with salad greens as soon as I arrive home; the lower terrace must usually wait until the end of June before it is dry enough to work. This year the lower garden was quite dry.

The breakup of the ice marks a profound change upon the land as well as the water. The moment the ice goes, the puddles in the forest suddenly disappear and spikes of green abruptly appear in the tangle of winter-brown sedges in the bogs. Rapidly the blue-tinged buds of the mountain marsh marigold thrust up through the marshy standing water and soon erupt into white, multiple-rayed blossoms. In sunny patches on the forest floor, little yellow violets bloom among the fallen pine needles. Within days this initial freshness is swallowed by the overpowering urge of every green thing to explode, and this delightful fragile changeover from winter into spring has disappeared. If I don't get home in time to observe it I feel cheated of an important part of my summer.

Hot, sunny weather usually means wind, but this June there was very little. Sometimes sultry-looking masses of vapour coalesced in

The garden

the east and distant thunder rumbled, but mostly the sun continued to shine out of a cloudless sky. The lake was often mirror calm, a rare event in summer. A week or so after I arrived, the pine trees blossomed. They rely on wind for reproduction—their pollen is produced in such quantities that it often blows like plumes of smoke from the trees. This year it fell into the water and clogged the shorelines thick as paint, swirled into fantastic abstract landscapes as it bent around the rocks. The spring blackflies, which are slightly larger than the fall ones (but still far smaller than their eastern counterparts), were the worst I'd ever experienced.

One morning I canoed up the lake to see if a tiny patch of northern anemones was in flower. I have found only three places in my area where this species grows and I did not yet have a good photo of it. Although it was still early in the day, it was already hot. Paddling up the lake, I could see all the hills and mountains perfectly reflected in the burnished mirror of the water. As soon as I pulled into the shore, the bugs pounced.

To catch the effect of the low morning sun shining through the delicate white petals of the anemone, I had to jam my cheek against the ground beside it, and it is not easy to take photos under those circumstances while hampered by a headnet. All too often I had to let the bugs have their way. As soon as I headed for home, a strong east wind jumped up from nowhere. I could see the wall of ruffled blue advancing toward me along the lake. East winds are generally not all that powerful, but this one made me work pretty hard in order to make headway. Winds from that direction in June often preclude thunder, but all day the sky stayed sharp and blue with never a cloud in sight. I heard later that Mary's resort at Nimpo had been visited by a freak windstorm that afternoon, during which ten trees blew over. It must have been very local as no one else was affected by it.

On June 24 I received a surprise visitor, the first person I had seen since my return home just over two weeks earlier. Like so many people who have summer cabins in the Nimpo Lake area, Ed was an American who owned a plane, and late in the morning his floats carved a white plume of spray on the motionless water. He had dropped by a number of times in previous years; this time he had just flown his son into Knot Lake in The Trench for a day's fishing. He would be picking the son up later; did I need anything from Nimpo? Having said I was fine but would appreciate a mail delivery if he really didn't mind, I gave him tea and a chunk of stone-oven bread, then went down to the wharf to see him off. He climbed aboard, pushing the plane away from the dock as he did so, and I caught the tail and swung the plane so that it pointed toward the channel between the islands. The aircraft drifted a couple of metres and Ed turned on the ignition. A clatter of motor, a cloud of blue smoke—and silence.

Northern anemone

More ignition whining, another brief burst from the engine, and then it cut out again. The third time it wouldn't fire at all.

Ed jumped onto the float, disengaged the paddle he kept strapped there and slowly brought the plane to within my reach, whereupon I held onto the mooring rope while he tried to fire up the engine again. "I can't understand it," he said. "I've just had the thing serviced and it was going really well. Not a sign of a problem on the way in." He was also worried about running his battery down—they were not designed to store a lot of power.

But eventually the motor fired and kept going. I released the rope, swung the tail again and, with some misgivings, watched him taxi through the channel and take off. I did not expect him back under the circumstances, but a few hours later he cruised in again, all smiles and bearing not only the promised mail but also a bag of fresh vegetables and fruit. He told me that the mechanical problem had been caused by excessively low air pressure generated by this freaky hot weather, and the fuel mix had been too rich. By the time he left to pick up his son, towering clouds were beginning to fall in on each other and I didn't envy him his bumpy flight. In the distance, thunder growled.

For a couple of weeks either side of the summer solstice, the sun sets far enough north to shine obliquely onto Monarch Mountain's face. That night the light had a strange orange cast and I knew there was a fire somewhere. But The Trench is a funnel for winds. In the past the mountains behind it had been thickly veiled with smoke when the source was way up in Alaska. I mentioned it to Rosemary in an email and she responded with news of the Turner Lake and Klinaklini strikes. Two nights later, I awoke shortly after midnight to smell smoke. Not the pleasant smoke of a winter blaze, but the acrid, wet smoke of burning green vegetation. It was unusually dark. Generally for the two months around the shortest night the sky retains a luminosity along the northern quarter of the horizon—not really daylight, but not quite dark either. Now, however, the night was a murky void so amorphous that I could not make out Kojo's Island barely 200 metres away. Periodic ghostly lightning switched on and off overhead like a silent neon sign. The smoke was alarming, but I tried to console myself that as no red glow was visible, whatever fire was thickening the air could not be too close. Toward dawn a small wind started from the west and I was at once relieved. West winds always cleared away inversion conditions, and thunder never came from that direction.

But daylight revealed a very peculiar world. Despite the persistent, steady breeze from the mountains, the lid of smog sat tight over the lake, eventually very slowly lifting a couple of hundred metres above the water. Monarch remained smothered, and even Louise O'Murphy was lopped off halfway up her flanks. From the low pass on the park boundary, through which the game route ran into The Trench, a bluish plume of smoke crawled like a snake, then proceeded to fan out toward me. Presumably it was issuing from the Turner Lake strike. Logic told me I could not be in any immediate danger—after all, the fire would have to cross The Trench before it got to Nuk Tessli, and there were several large lakes in between us. But I wondered how John Edwards was making out at Lonesome Lake. If I was getting smoke problems up here, it must be pretty bad down at his place.

Despite my brain telling me all was well, the constant dry lightning and now this strange, smoky gloom made me nervous enough to think about organizing an escape plan in case fire danger became a fact. How far away would one have to go from it to be safe? If a fire came down one side of the lake, was the water wide enough to protect me? Much of the shoreline forest comprised stands of lodgepole, a comparatively fast-growing pine species, but the bigger islands, even though they were fairly close to the shore, were almost exclusively covered in large, mature specimens of the much slower-growing whitebark pine. Logging activities had shown me that these large trees might be between 300 and 500 years old and the lodgepole stands probably no more than 150 years old; presumably these old whitebarks on the islands had survived at least one major conflagration.

I found a mouse-proof container (which happened to be a

cooler in which Rosemary had packed some homegrown greens that had been flown in on one of the manuscript flights during the winter) and placed in it three days' food for both me and my dogs. Figuring that if worse came to the worst I would cross the lake in a canoe, I added important documents such as manuscript drafts, journals and financial papers, as well as my camera and exposed film. On top was a list of other vital items, like the computer, which I could not pack right away as I needed to keep using it. Beside the cooler sat the dog packs and my backpack loaded with camping gear—spare clothes, billy cans, tent, matches and candles (the latter seemed bizarre under the circumstances but I have known hot, violent thunderstorms to end in heavy hail and snow on more than one occasion), and a second list of items I would take if I flew out and had more time and space to organize things—chainsaw and other expensive tools, photo albums, the large carton of snail-mail correspondence from which I drew mailing lists to advertise slide show tours, and so on. Presumably a building would burn all the more readily if flammable materials were stored in it, so gas, chain and two-stroke oil, household paints, fibreglass resin, kerosene and metal cans of cooking oil were packed over to the old foodstore, a wooden crate of poles I had built when I was still living in a tent and constructing my first cabin. Bears like gas just as much as food and will often destroy a plastic gas can with their claws in an effort to get at the contents. Two of the poles on the lid, I noticed, were rotten and broken, but I didn't think a bear could get in yet. Chainsaws, matches, candles, kerosene lamps and other flammables that had to be kept dry were taken to Cabin One. It stood a little apart from the other two, and I figured that if the worst happened, it was the structure I could most afford to lose.

Not that I could really contemplate the loss of any of these buildings . . . I had spent every penny I earned in the last two decades creating this life in the wilderness. Fire insurance had never been an option: Spinster Lake was so far from any kind of fire-protection system that the fees would have been astronomical. I had absolutely no monetary assets apart from these structures, and even if the forest around the lake remained untouched, I'd already scrounged far and wide for materials to construct the three existing cabins, and there would not be much usable timber left for starting again. In any case, if everything was burnt, who would want to spend any money to come here? I had no place to go outside Nuk Tessli, only the rough little cabin in which I camped as I passed back and forth through Nimpo Lake, and that was never a place I could contemplate using as a permanent home.

By the end of the day, the overcast had lifted, but the wind had backed and was coming from the east again. The sky above Fish Lake blackened, and soon Halfway Mountain was obliterated by massed piles of stygian vapour laced with jagged electrical flashes. Violent afternoon storms and flickering nights were now becoming a way of life. On June 27 I heard on the radio that there had been 1,400 lightning strikes in British Columbia over the previous 24 hours, and 400 fires were now burning throughout the province.

As well as the fire, the lightning storms were also causing me concern regarding a hike I had planned for the beginning of July. I had arranged, once again, to meet wwoofers at Top Lake at the head of Maydoe Creek. Two Canadian women, Stephanie and Katherine, had come to one of my slide shows in Alberta and they seemed experienced and practical in the bush. They had finished school in Ontario and were due to start teaching with the Voluntary Service Overseas, in Ghana, in September. The third wwoofer was a Spanish male whose English was almost non-existent—I only hoped he had understood my emails sufficiently to realize what he had to do and bring. Vicente was to stay at Nuk Tessli for ten days, but the two women planned to leave at the end of the month so that Stephanie could take a course as part of her training for Ghana.

Stephanie had a car, and using the miracle of email I had been able to arrange for the two women to pick up Vicente en route, drive to the end of the road at the east end of Charlotte Lake and, with the aid of instructions and maps I had left for them at the Nimpo cabin, guide him through the tangle of brush and swamp to Top Lake. Top Lake, however, was at the edge of the alpine, tucked under the north face of Halfway Mountain—right where the daily storms were now the most violent. I had experienced a terrible storm in that valley once, a horrifying cacophony of bangs and flashes, both occurring every few seconds with no apparent relationship to each other. It continued for well over an hour before adding violent hail to its repertoire. Having smashed my camp, the precipitation turned to torrential rain followed by several centimetres of snow. This was during the first week of August. No doubt the narrow valley with its steep, rocky walls had made the storm seem more intense than it was, but to suggest that we deliberately seek those conditions as a meeting point was stupid. But how to get hold of Stephanie and Katherine to cancel the trip? Both wwoofers had email addresses, but they were already en route and probably would not check email very often. And then my own email packed up: it was during this dark time that I discovered my deep-cycle batteries were no longer functioning properly. I had also been warned that thick cloud cover could cut me off from the satellite, and for three excessively dark and smoky days I could neither send nor receive.

But a day or two before the expedition was to take place, the weather finally cooled and it even dribbled a bit of rain. I contacted Mary by radiophone and told her the hike was going ahead as planned. The only thing now was to hope that we did not have another Naomi and Scott debacle.

I need not have worried. The three wwoofers arrived long before dark on the appointed day, Stephanie and Katherine in well-used Canadian gear and Vicente with equally worn equipment but dressed in coarse white cotton like a Colombian Indian. The brush and swamps had been miserable, and in the drizzly weather the bugs had been at their worst, but the trio had made very good time and I assured them that the hiking would improve. The rest of the hike was muggy and very buggy, but otherwise without incident.

The first paying guests arrived not long after the wwoofers, and the promised busy tourist season began. The weather remained mostly dull with occasional sprinkles of rain and varying degrees of smoke, but we had some quite nice days. I have a photo of that time, in which four guests are standing in summer shirts and sleeveless blouses on top of the North Ridge, with flowers at their feet and a panorama of the Coast Range behind them. There is hardly any smoke in the picture at all.

CHAPTER 15

The Lonesome Lake Fire

ALL ALONE AT LONESOME LAKE
An animal lover's last stand
by Mark Hume

The last stand at Lonesome Lake began yesterday for John Edwards, 77, when he trekked back to the isolated homestead his family has occupied for nearly 100 years in north-western British Columbia. Far beyond the end of the last road, in a remote valley filled with smoke, with a forest fire roaring so loud it wakes him at night, Mr. Edwards has returned to the wilderness to be with the animals he loves until the last moment.

"I want to be there at the end," he says, sobbing into a telephone line hissing with static, as he calls from Hagensborg, in the Bella Coola Valley. "The foxes, squirrels and martens have been my only companions all these years. They are like family to me.

"Excuse me, excuse me," he says, apologizing for his tears, "I'm breaking up. To me, it's like watching your children burn" . . .

—Globe and Mail, *Saturday, July 24, 2004*

On July 25, a month and a day after the Turner Lake lightning strike, a party of three paying guests flew into Nuk Tessli. It was late afternoon and a southwest wind was gusting strongly, a condition that is very common during hot weather in summer. All day I had watched the fire clouds building up over the Klinaklini; these could be seen behind Kojo's Island through the lowest gap in the southern horizon. Contrary to what one might expect, forest-fire clouds are white and look like tight piles of cumulonimbus; they are created by the steam that is released from burning vegetation and are quite different from the more sluggish brown smoke clouds, which arrange themselves in layers and usually lie closer to the ground. The brown plume from the Klinaklini fire, driven by the strong ground wind, rolled due north like a rooster-tail dust cloud on a country road, but at Nuk Tessli, the fresh wind had cleared the smoke from the mountains beautifully and the world was blue and shining.

The northern quarter of the landscape is hidden from me when I am in the cabin or on the decks, and it was not until I heard the plane coming and went down to the wharf to meet it that I became aware of another monstrous fire cloud, this one towering over the North Ridge. It was piled in tight white billows hundreds of metres high. It must have been coming from the Turner Lake fire—but it didn't seem to be in the right place. I could have sworn that it had moved farther north—or was my poor sense of direction merely confusing the issue?

The plane deposited three visitors who were bubbling over with excitement. The smoke from the Klinaklini fire had been so thick where it had crossed Highway 20, there was concern that the road might be closed and they had not been sure if they were going to make it to Nimpo. I asked the pilot about the fire cloud behind me, but he assured me the blaze was still a good distance away and my place could not possibly be in danger. The Hunlen Falls area, which was close to the original strike, had been closed and everyone evacuated from it, which was a blow to Tweedsmuir Air as they not only fly in a large number of people to see Hunlen Falls, they also manage the campgrounds and rent canoes for people who wish to paddle farther along the Turner Lake chain. The area had been closed for a time after the initial strike, but opened again during the cooler, slightly damper weather; now the situation was far more serious.

As the afternoon waned, smoke began to accumulate behind the gap in the hills toward Nimpo through which the plane had so recently flown. This was closer to home than the fire cloud had been and consequently more alarming. The sky remained perfectly clear at Nuk Tessli, and the lowering sun shone golden rays toward the smoke, lighting the alpine areas of the hills so brightly they looked, against the black darkness of the sky, as if they were covered in snow. The top of the smoke cloud was a sunset-coloured cauldron of orange and brown.

I radiophoned Stewarts; the connection was poor but Rhonda, Duncan's wife, said they were very glad I had contacted them because a Forestry helicopter was visiting all the resorts in the Charlotte Alplands and advising everyone to evacuate. Their two cabins, one in the valley north of mine and the other two lakes downriver from my own, were already empty. Rhonda told me to keep in touch by email. I informed my guests of the decision—the three tourists had barely unpacked, and Stephanie and Katherine, who had been away on a three-day hike, had very little to put together, so their efforts did not take long. My emergency escape kit was still sitting on the floor where I had put it together a month before, but several of the items had been used and moved. Fortunately the lists were still with the boxes and it was not hard to get everything organized again. There were also the large cartons of fruit and other produce that the clients had brought with them. If we had to leave and the place did not burn, the produce would rot and the cabin would be a magnet for hungry bears: in the end I resolved that if there was room we would take the produce with us. It seemed stupid when so much of value would be left behind, but I simply could not make a choice among all the other items in my possession. If the produce could not be flown out, it would be dumped well out into the lake where anything that didn't sink would be blown to areas well away from the cabins. Any bears that might be around would, I reasoned, be attracted to it rather than my buildings. (This is not something I would ever do under normal circumstances, but extreme situations write their own code of behaviour.)

By now it was time to think about supper and I wondered whether or not to cook a meal. I contacted Stewarts again; the earliest they could come for us was 7:00 p.m., an hour and a half ahead. There still had been no sign of the promised helicopter. We threw together a soup to go with that morning's fresh-baked bread. All five visitors were brimming with excitement and their voices rang shrilly and delightedly as they wolfed down their meal. I, however, could hardly eat a thing. My stomach was clenched in knots—all I could feel was dread. What on earth would I do if Nuk Tessli burned?

Several small planes had cruised overhead at different times— no doubt locals going to check out the fire. Then, while we were eating, we heard the rattle of a helicopter. At once I tied the dogs and started to run toward the small meadow behind the cabins. I have cleared a couple of small trees to make a landing pad for just such emergencies as this. But the chopper merely circled round a couple of times—I could see faces staring at us out of the windows—and kept heading straight toward the fire.

Seven o'clock came and went. Stewarts were not answering their emails (they are not habituated to computers and use them only as a necessary evil). I could not raise them by radiophone, so I switched to the private local channel in an effort to call Mary. The phone was answered at once by Terry Brandt, Mary's neighbour, who said Mary and friends were up at Wilderness Lake. He, Terry, was standing by to help coordinate evacuees. He had flown over the fire a couple of hours ago—his would have been one of the planes we had heard. The fire had crossed The Trench at the head of Lonesome Lake, somewhere in the region of John Edwards' homestead, and was now racing up the Atnarko. The fire cloud had indeed moved; that put it two valleys north of my place, but I could not be in any danger. John and a group of firefighters had been down there trying to set up sprinklers but the fire had suddenly leapt the river and they'd had to leave in a hurry. The old Edwards homestead had likely been consumed. There had been too much smoke when Terry had flown over to assess the full extent of the damage, but he could not imagine that any of the buildings down there would have survived.

I must confess that the full horror of John's loss did not have much impact on me at first. The assurance that Nuk Tessli was still safe was all the news I could assimilate. In the meantime, in the clear sky to the west, the sun was dropping close to the horizon. There was still no sign of Stewarts' plane. I asked Terry if he would mind land-phoning them to see if in fact they were still planning on coming in, which he did. No, came the eventual reply, Tweedsmuir Air would not be picking us up that night. We were, however, to remain on evacuation alert. Did we want them to come in the morning? Terry reiterated that we were still a long way from the fire, and I said I would see how everyone felt the next day.

So once again the visitors unpacked. Gleefully, they gathered to watch the towering fire cloud blush red with the light from the dying sun, and day one of our fire ordeal was over.

CHAPTER 16

John Edwards' Story

From*: Rosemary*
To*: Chris Czajkowski*
Sent*: Sunday, July 25, 2004, 9:58 a.m.*
Subject*: Fire Update*

Just had a long chat with John Edwards, who is out at Stewarts. There are now three fires; one down by his place, one on the west side of Lonesome and one down on the north end. The fire suppression folk have finally put in extensive ground crews at the north end, and also helicopter pads. Still no water bombers, in fact the only water bomber was last June 22nd when they did 3 sides of the initial fire, which was up on the flat by Turner. They didn't bother doing the steep talus slope down toward Lonesome. They returned home with retardant still in the planes (John was monitoring the air traffic conversation). Of course, the fire jumped down very quickly.

Poor John is so distressed. He told me about his little fox and the other animals that have become his friends. He also warned us to be very alert as the fire could be in The Precipice very quickly. It is on the north side of Trumpeter Mountain already, and there are only about 40 kms of rolling uninterrupted forest between us with no lakes to block it. It only needs the wind to shift a point or two to drive the fire right our way.

John went to the Bella Coola Valley newspaper, and the result is the Globe and Mail article I am attaching to you. This morning on

CBC we were told that "fire crews are mopping up the Lonesome Lake fire"—a total lie.

Did I mention that the Klinaklini fire is a class 5 fire? It is taking out Schilling Lake: there are 5 or 6 families affected by it. It is now over 1,200 hectares. The Lonesome Lake fire is slated as the highest danger of all—class 6.

To reach the Atnarko, a valley running more or less parallel to mine about 16 kilometres north, the fire must have gone through the Turners' property, as well as the old homestead at Lonesome Lake; by inference, my first cabin would also have been consumed. This news produced only a momentary pang at the time; I was far too concerned about Spinster Lake. The Turners had left the valley not long after I did, so they would not have lost their actual home, although I am sure the destruction of the property and its surroundings would upset them greatly—so much of their life had been spent there. But I had been at that cabin for only four years and, whereas I had experienced great times and learned a huge amount, it was no longer part of my life. Its destiny had been to rot back into the forest, and the fire meant that it had simply disintegrated sooner.

But poor John. His whole life was down there. He had been so proud of the old house, which his family had moved into nearly eighty years ago when he was an infant because their original cabin burned down. John's life, it appears, has been bracketed by fire. The old homestead, in which I had stayed when I house-sat for John so that he could go out for his brother's funeral, had been stuffed with artifacts and books and documents detailing both John's and his father's animal research and his family's esoteric occupation of the area. John worked outside for a while when he was younger, but he has lived down there, mostly on his own, these last two decades, and has been slowly and lovingly restoring the old building.

It was only when I read the newspaper articles (which were emailed to me by friends) that I came to understand how much of a nightmare this last month had been for John. While we were

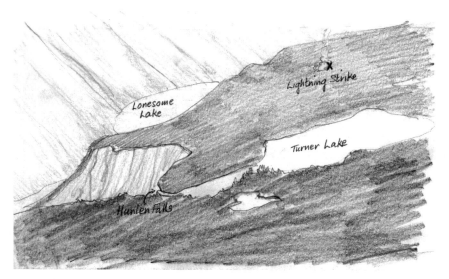

grumbling about poor visibility, John was trying to salvage everything of importance to him.

The strike occurred on the comparatively flat plateau between the east shore of Turner Lake and the steep drop-off toward Lonesome Lake. A few buckets of retardant were dropped at that time, but no one made any real effort to put it out. Sure, the fire seemed insignificant and the weather turned dampish, but as the *Coast Mountain News* reported, because of its proximity to Hunlen Falls, a tourist-dollar earner, it was in a fire-suppression zone. Officials cited danger to personnel, but when one looks at the location of the small puff of smoke on a photograph taken two days after the initial strike (posted on the BC Forest Service website), one cannot see why the danger to firefighters was deemed so extreme at the time.

Once the fire crept over the rim of the valley and started to fizz and spot its way down the very steep wall to Lonesome Lake, however, that was indeed a different matter. John kept begging and pleading with Parks and Forestry officials to do something, but to no avail. Rumour had it that the two ministries could not agree on how to tackle the situation or who should pay for it, so nothing was done. They denied this vociferously, of course. John began to make trips to the road with valued documents. He had to undertake two boat rides and two 4-kilometre hikes to reach his truck; therefore, on each trip he could take no more than what he could carry on his back.

On his last hike, John carried out his chainsaw and other necessary tools. By then he could hear the fire roaring day and night, and even feel the heat of the flames. A crew of firefighters was helicoptered in with John to try to set up sprinklers—remarkably effective lines of hoses that are fed by a gas pump and that can run for 24 hours. But before the crew could get them working, the fire suddenly leapt the narrow stretch of river near the head of the homestead. The men piled aboard the choppers and took off, escaping by the skin of their teeth and leaving John's life's work to the flames.

CHAPTER 17

July 26 to 28

From: *Chris Czajkowski*
To: *Herbert*
Sent: *Monday, July 26, 2004, 6:01 a.m.*
Subject: *We're still here*
Hullo Herbert,

So the fire has hit the Lower Mainland news! In response to your query as to whether or not your group will still be able to come for your scheduled tour next Wednesday—I am afraid I cannot say. I was told to evacuate my guests last night but no one came to pick us up and at sundown I found that the fire was still two valleys north of my place. This morning a haze of smoke covers most of the sky but it is still crystal clear in the south.

I'll keep you posted.

From: *Chris Czajkowski*
To: *fly@tweedsmuirair.com*
Sent: *Monday, July 26, 2004, 6:02 a.m.*
Subject: *Visibility*

Hazy ceiling of smoke about 2,500 feet above the lake but lifting. Monarch etc is socked in but Wilderness Mountain in the south is crystal clear.

The clients aren't out of bed yet. I'll let you know what they want to do as soon as I can.

From*: Tweedsmuir Air*
To*: Chris Czajkowski*
Sent*: Tuesday, July 27, 2004, 12:04 p.m.*
Subject*: rcmp message*
Hello Chris

This is glenn ramsay from the anahim lk rcmp . . . we had to evacuate the charlotte lake area as you know and we were just checking on your status . . . please liaise with terry on radio if you need anything regarding an emergency vac . . .

I have an inquiry with you about an abandoned ontario plated mazda protégé vehicle on the southwest side of charlotte lk . . . the vehicle is locked and it appears that they may have hiked up into the mountains . . . maybe to your cabin??? . . . do you know anything about the ontario plated vehicle and a lady by the name of stephanie jane hammond of thunder bay ontario . . .

The clients, to my relief, decided to stay. One more day and I would not have to return any of their deposit. The major expense I had incurred by setting up the satellite system was never far from my mind. Every day these current clients stayed would help to pay my bills.

In fact, July 26 was not at all dramatic for us in any way. The wind began to die down and the atmosphere stayed fairly clear—the clients had no idea that the smoggy-looking mountains they were looking at were only the foreground ranges until I showed them the photographs in my albums.

I had to work at keeping a cheery note to the proceedings—the clients had not come to see my long face—but the worry was not going to go away. I was now concerned to see that the wind was slowly veering during the day. Every time I looked at the smoke-hazed clouds, I could see that the wind direction had swung farther north. A clockwise change from southwest to north always produces calmer weather, and the drop in wind strength was soon very marked; this would be a big help in reducing the ferocity of the fire, but I wondered what it would do to the smoke. At sundown, the wall of orange and black built up again in the gap in the hills toward Nimpo—much higher this time. If the wind continued to veer, it would start blowing that smoke straight toward us.

Which is exactly what did happen.

I had little satisfaction in being proved right.

Day three of the fire could not be described as anything but eerie. At first light, some of the landforms could still be seen, but the sun rose as a blood red disk that one could stare full in the eye, and its reflection made slow, sliding patterns on the almost motionless water. Later, both sun and landforms disappeared entirely. The air was thick and acrid, and it became absolutely motionless. A fine sifting of white ash fell and the gloom intensified to a kind of brown twilight, which I found as oppressive as any other aspect of the whole business. Even the moths were fooled. All day they batted against the windows as they do in the evening before a rain. But my bones did not ache in the right way, so I knew the atmospheric pressure was still high. According to the weather websites, it was another brilliantly sunny 30°C day outside the smoke, but under this heavy pall it was cool enough to wear a sweater.

Stephanie and Katherine went up the two lakes with the clients, who set off happily enough with a fishing pole, announcing that they were going to hold their catch up in the air on their way back so that the fish would arrive already smoked. A bit of time to myself is of great value to me in the summer, but once the chores had been done and the numerous emails of concern from strangers as well as friends had been answered, being alone was perhaps not the best thing on this occasion, for all I could do was brood. It was mightily fortunate that the clients were enjoying the venture, for unbeknownst to them, they could not have flown out if they wished to, probably not even with a helicopter. If they had realized this, their attitude toward their stay would have changed completely.

The oddest feature of the day was the periodic distant rumble of what sounded like a cat. The only vehicular sounds I ever hear come from aircraft. (Snow machines used to visit in the winter when the trappers were working, but that operation has long since ceased to be economical this far off the road, and the trek in here on those machines is far too much work for recreationists.) Once in a while I caught the rattle of a helicopter, but the overpowering noise seemed to be the cat. I could not imagine where the machine could be operating. If it was working along the Atnarko, close to the fire, the two mountain ridges would block the sound. But it was no figment of my imagination, for the clients had heard it, too. It has been suggested that perhaps the smoke funnelled the sound, as cloud certainly does, but cloud has that ability because it is composed of water. The smoke, or possibly the fine rain of ash, dampened sounds as snow does: the sound of the occasional high-altitude aircraft passing overhead was muffled, and even our voices were flattened and hushed. By mid-afternoon, even the cat noises had ceased. The silence was eerie. The canoeists arrived home fishless but like bright ghosts in their orange life vests and welded to their strong reflections,

Stephanie and Katherine in the canoe

mirrored images that hung suspended in a totally featureless brown, gloomy void.

By evening there was a very slight clearing, and the whole world turned a very strange pink. Everything—air, trees, buildings, people—was suffused with this rosy cast. I had the radiophone on quite a lot of the time (though my solar-powered batteries were losing their charge in this smog) and learned from various conversations that Mary and her friends were still up at Wilderness Lake. Visibility up there had been up to 8 kilometres for most of the day so it had not been considered a problem, although if they had needed to fly out, they would have had to go the long way around, via Hunlen Falls, to avoid the smoke. Wilderness Lake is about 200 metres higher in altitude and 10 kilometres south of mine.

The clients' morale was finally, and very understandably, beginning to flag. I emailed Tweedsmuir Air on their behalf, saying that they might want to leave a day earlier than scheduled and asking if Stewarts could be ready to pick them up the following morning if need be. The clients might still change their minds if the smoke cleared, and I promised to contact them as soon as the decision had been made.

As the 28th of July dawned, however, we might have been in a different country. A few soft scarves of smoke lay across Monarch's face, but the snowfields shone serenely in the soft pink and orange light of the smoke-filtered sunrise, a pretty enough prospect that I got the clients out of bed to see it. The smoke thickened a little as the sun climbed higher—a really clear day was too much to expect—but it all looked so benign that the clients decided to stay after all, and we set off on a hike to the North Ridge. The flowers would normally have been at their best up there at this time of year, but the droughts of this and previous years had produced a poor showing. Still, there were a good number and the hazy sunlight was a photographer's dream, for it made the flowers' colours glow like stained glass.

I was hoping to see something of the fire activity once we got to the top of the ridge, but although we heard an occasional helicopter, there was very little sign of life. The valley between us and the fire was green and silent. There was little wind and no fire cloud behind the far ridge, and most of the sluggish slabs of smoke that crawled from the fire site were heading toward The Precipice. Even as we watched, however, skeins of smoke began to fan out our way and the tenuous sunlight faded to dreariness once again.

As we started down, I noticed a movement on the tundra. At first I thought it must be a furry black caterpillar, but it was a cone hanging onto a bit of heather, blowing slightly in the barely noticeable breeze. It was probably a spruce cone, burnt to a black cinder, light as smoke. It must have been carried on the fire wind clean across two mountain ridges and an unspoiled valley. It was scary to think that potentially flammable material could travel so far.

The smoke was thickening fast, but we were in the trees before it became too ominous. Right around the time we arrived home, I heard a Beaver heading toward Wilderness Lake and knew that Mary and her friends would be flying out as scheduled. One of the couples had a plane of their own, and their practice was to finish cleaning the cabin and fly out about an hour later. I heard them take off and turn north toward Nimpo. They flew back and forth a time or two and I remember thinking that the smoke must have been thinner up there, for visibility was already quite bad by my cabins: I assumed they were circling to get a better look at the fire. Later I found out that they had in fact got caught up in the smoke and had quite a fright before they managed to find their way through.

That same day, John Edwards, his sister Trudy, her husband Jack and their daughter Susan had been flown in by the press to be photographed among the ruins of their homesteads. The buildings were nothing but a devastation of ash and heat-distorted metal. Not a scrap of wood remained. It was almost as if the fire had had special dispensation to raze the buildings to the ground, for it had spotted among the forest, and there were trees close to the buildings that had not been burned at all. John found his vegetable garden, which had been in a cleared space, still intact. "I must be the only person who has ever baked his potatoes before he harvested them," he was reported in the *Vancouver Sun* to have said bitterly.

CHAPTER 18

The Lonesome Lake Fire, Day Five

From*: R.S.*
To*: Chris Czajkowski*
Sent*: Tuesday, July 27, 2004, 8:59 p.m.*
Subject*: Interview*
Chris

Our newspaper is interested in interviewing you and getting your experiences and eagle-eye view of the fires near you. . .

If you have a satellite phone, perhaps you could call me when you get this Tuesday night. I know it's late (9 p.m.), but we are putting the second edition of our newspaper out at 11:00 p.m. (2 hours from now). . .

If email is the only option, maybe you would be interested in writing something down on what you see and why you are staying there and your fears of evacuation.

But please first try and give me a call. . .

R.S.
Reporter
The Province

From: *Chris Czajkowski*
To: *R.S.*
Sent: *Wednesday, July 28, 2004, 6:59 a.m.*

Subject: *re: Interview*
Hi R.S.

Sorry, although I downloaded at about 9:00 p.m. last night, I did not receive your message until this morning. I don't have a reliable phone so will have to correspond with you in this way.

This is what has happened so far . . .

The current clients are due to leave today. The smoke was pretty thick earlier but now it is a little clearer and I think a plane can get in. To answer your question, my two friends, two dogs and I will stay until it becomes either too dangerous or too uncomfortable. We are perfectly safe but I need hardly say that this whole situation is very serious and nerve-wracking for me.

If you want more information . . . I will check the email every couple of hours or so. I don't leave the computer on full time as I operate on solar power, and with all this smoke around, my batteries are not getting enough sun.

From: *R.S.*
To: *Chris Czajkowski*
Sent: *Wednesday, July 28, 2004, 12:06 p.m.*
Subject: *re: Interview*
Chris

Thanks so much for the email, I appreciate the quick response . . .

We're hoping we can get this into tomorrow's paper (Thursday) to help put a human face and story behind the fire, much like John Edwards and the unfortunate impact the fire had on him. I talked to John the other day and, while I think he was a bit numb, he emphasized the fact that he's "a survivor." Do you feel the same way about yourself?

From: *Chris Czajkowski*
To: *Rosemary Neads*
Sent: *Wednesday, July 28, 2004, 11:47 p.m.*
Subject: *How are you?*

Smoke too thick for the clients to fly out this a.m. as scheduled.

They look a bit taken aback. So far it's been a big adventure, but as soon as their plans are disrupted. . .

The two wwoofers are happy to hang on and work for a few more days. All the clients for the next two weeks have cancelled, but there is always a lot of stuff to do. We may all end up going out together if things do not improve. Trouble is, if conditions improve enough to fly, then you want to stay. . .

Around noon, the mountains began to emerge very slowly. At first, strange, disembodied patches of light appeared floating above the far end of the lake. It was necessary to strain one's eyes to see them, but the patches gradually turned into sunlit snowfields.

Stewarts had tried to get in at the scheduled time of 10:00 a.m. to pick up the clients but had been turned back. A small peak to the north of Spinster Lake is my usual mark for visibility in that direction, and when it emerged, albeit very hazily, I gave Stewarts a call to say that things were improving at my end, and they were finally able to get a plane in during the middle of the afternoon. The clients would not be able to reach Williams Lake airport in time for their scheduled flight to the Coast, but Pacific Coastal Airlines, which runs many of the backcountry services in the west, and which handled the *Spotted Dick* manuscript so efficiently, has never forgotten its bush-charter origins. They kindly said that under the circumstances they would not charge the clients any extra to reschedule their flight.

It was a very strange feeling. Apart from Stephanie and Katherine, and whatever firefighters might be working, there was not a single human being left in the area for 50 kilometres in any direction. No tourists at Hunlen Falls, no families down the Klinaklini, no one at Charlotte Lake (more than a hundred buildings are scattered along the shore there, mostly summer cabins, though by no means would all of them have been occupied) and poor John, of course, had been burned out. My own clients had left and all future ones had cancelled, so that worry had been taken away, and as the air began to clear my spirits lifted with it. There was a great feeling of freedom, as if a huge weight had been lifted off my shoulders.

It was so glorious, so euphoric, to see the mountains sharpen and become clear and to see the sky turn blue again. The light on the wind-ruffled water sparkled white and bright, instead of being dulled with the orange or brown haze we had lived with for so long. The breeze was persistent, but comparatively gentle. It was an absolutely perfect summer afternoon. As the sun circled round the sky and began to drop toward the northwest, I was somewhat disappointed to notice that it was being met by a few tendrils of smoke that were beginning to creep from behind the North Ridge. I still thought nothing of it: the mountains above the head of the lake were sharp as diamonds and our world was beautiful and serene.

It did not occur to me to look north, but when I took a hike to the outhouse I was confronted with that quarter of the landscape and received a great shock. A solid-looking black wall of smoke reared behind Avalanche Lake Lookout. This was a far greater mass than any we had previously seen, and when we looked a short time later, it had grown horrifically into a tottering black tower that was beginning to curl ominously over the top of Nuk Tessli. Two things were particularly worrisome about this smoke pall: one was that it appeared to be travelling against the prevailing wind, and the other—even more disturbing—was that the lower part of it, the area tight against the North Ridge, was glowing orange.

We had often seen smoke tinted reds and pinks by a lowering sun, but this was different. The colour was at the bottom, not the top. The light that caused it came not from the sun, but from flames. This meant that either the flames were monstrously high, or the fire had jumped into the next valley and was about to climb over the North Ridge into mine. A soft, insidious rain of white ash began to fall.

I called Terry on the radiophone, and he answered at once. "Do you know what is happening?" I asked.

"Nobody can tell from this end," he replied. "There's too much smoke for anyone to see anything. All we know is that it is something big."

I suppose we could have tried to weather this next crisis, but it was suddenly all too much. Even if the fire did not reach us, it looked as though the smoke was going to be another nightmare. Apart from the discomfort and misery of it, there was the problem of getting the two wwoofers out. Stephanie was due to fly from Vancouver to her course in less than a week, so there was a deadline we had to meet.

Smoke cloud over the North Ridge

Of the three overland routes we might have taken, two took us either into the evacuated area at Charlotte Lake or directly into the fire zone in The Trench. The third would have been a longer trip south down the McClinchy, into which Fish Lake disgorges—doable, but there was only one lake of any size in that direction and I worried about travelling so far from a large body of water. As we had already seen, if the fire really got going, it could travel much faster than we could.

"I think we'd better get out of here," I said. "Can you ask Stewarts if they can come in? Tell Duncan there're three people and the two dogs."

Terry called Stewarts and reported that they would be leaving right away so should be there within thirty minutes. During our frantic rush to re-collect our bail-out boxes and packages (this time dismantling the computer, and our uneaten supper was ladled into canning jars and thrown into the box of produce, along with the remaining bread), I checked the North Ridge every few seconds. Despite tendrils of smoke around its farther edge, Avalanche Mountain remained visible. The intensity of the glow at the bottom of the smoke pall had diminished somewhat, but now, although the mountains in the west were still shining brightly, a sick light pervaded Nuk Tessli. The water was orange, the foliage a dark, corpse-like green and the tree branches as pale as weathered bones.

Once again there was the horrible indecision as to what extra items to take. In the end I could not single out any of my beloved objects. Even the chainsaw was left behind—I didn't think I would have time to organize the tools and I wasn't at all sure there would be room in the plane.

For all the last-minute panic, we were standing waiting on the dock for several minutes before the plane came in. I had expected the pilot to go the long way around, for the Avalanche Lake valley, the usual route to Nimpo, was already thick with smoke, but to my surprise the plane emerged right out of the gloom.

Two pilots came with it. "Don't worry!" they said. "The fire is still a long way from this place."

Despite their attempts to allay my fears, they were not about to hang around and they loaded us all up quickly. Doug, the one doing the flying, was allergic to dogs, and he put me in the back seat with my animals, whence both promptly tried to climb on my lap. Katherine was given the best place to take photos, as she was the most experienced with a camera. My camera was also with me on the plane, but what with the dogs, my phobia of flying and all the other trauma, I had no heart to use it.

We took off into the wind toward the shining mountains, but then curved back and plunged into the eerie fog of the smoke. Visibility got poorer and poorer, but the pilots didn't seem worried. After an interminable time (the whole flight is only twenty minutes, but to someone with a phobia it seems endless) we became aware of a glitter of red in the gloom. It was a flame slightly to the right of our course. As we came around the edge of Avalanche Mountain, we were suddenly presented with a ragged, smoking, burning line of fire stretching diagonally up the far side of the next valley, its lower end anchored against Crazy Bear Lake. The fire was now 12 kilometres from Nuk Tessli, a considerably shorter distance than it had travelled in the two days after wiping out the Edwards homestead. There was a lodge at the northern end of Crazy Bear Lake. The tourists had long since been evacuated and a line of sprinklers had been installed; but I could not see how anything in this vastly burning world could possibly be saved.

Slowly we bumped along in the heated air (although it was actually less turbulent than I had expected). More scattered clumps of fire, then through the gloom we came upon another burning lake. This would have been Little Charlotte at the head of the Atnarko, where it runs out of Charlotte Lake. The whole shoreline was on fire with flames as high as trees. The pilots told us, however, that when they had flown in, they estimated the height of the conflagration to be 150 metres. That is what created that terrifying orange glow we had seen above the North Ridge.

From Little Charlotte we could look right down the Atnarko to The Trench. Below the lid of smoke, as at the end of a long tunnel, the mountains still shone blue and white and clear.

Suddenly we were tossed into the air like a ping-pong ball. The plane must have hit the heat turbulence from the fire. It was a horrifying sensation, but in an instant we were through it and into the comparative clarity of the north shore of Charlotte Lake.

The long smoke cloud had a solid edge here, and it plumed over the length of the lake and beyond, blanketing the long line of deserted summer homes. Somewhere under the pall was Stephanie's car: an evacuation order means no one is allowed in under any circumstances, and we wondered if we would be allowed to retrieve it. Trumpeter Mountain at the west end of the lake was burning, but several fire roads had been plowed through there, the last of which reached to the treeline in an effort to save the Charlotte Lake settlement. Later it was found that the fire was jumping the first line of defence even as we flew over, but there were still two more fire roads to go.

But now we were over the flatter Chilcotin, and bathed in sunshine. At Nimpo Lake, when we landed, it was a beautiful, golden evening. It was so calm and serene and trauma-free that it was bewildering, as if we had been transported to a different planet.

Charlotte Lake and the smoke cloud

But when we looked back the way we had come, the foothills and mountains one can normally see from Stewarts float-plane dock were swallowed up in a great black wall of nothing.

CHAPTER 19

Evacuation

RESIDENTS FLEEING HUGE FIRE FURIOUS WITH FORESTRY OFFICIALS

"If you're not going to defend our home, let us go back and defend it ourselves."

by Jeff Lee and Amy O'Brien

NIMPO LAKE—The raging Lonesome Lake fire nearly tripled in size Tuesday as hot, dry winds continued to fan the flames and push the blaze toward homes and a resort east of Tweedsmuir Park.

The fire exploded last weekend after extreme heat and wind rushed through the area, but it had been burning for more than a month before it ripped through the park toward Charlotte Lake and Anahim Lake.

The blaze grew to 10,300 hectares, or 103 square kilometres Tuesday. A day earlier, it was 3,700 hectares and last Friday covered just 550 hectares.

—Front page, *Vancouver Sun*, Wednesday, July 28, 2004

BLAZE WASN'T FOUGHT QUICKLY ENOUGH, RESIDENTS COMPLAIN

"My whole life is here," says wilderness author who fears for her home

by Rob Shaw and Damian Inwood, Staff Reporters

A well-known Canadian author living near Tweedsmuir Provincial

Park says she won't leave her home threatened by raging forest fires until she absolutely has to.

"My whole life is here—I have no other home—it has taken me 15 years to get a measure of comfort here, and this lifestyle produces so little income that I would have no capital or resources to start again," said best-selling author Chris Czajkowski . . .

—*Province*, Thursday, July 29, 2004

There was, Duncan informed me as I went to pay for our emergency flight, a community debriefing at 9:00 p.m. at the new recreation centre on the reserve at Anahim Lake. It was already 8:00 p.m.; because I was so unused to looking at clocks and the sun was still shining, I had no idea it was so late. We drove to the cabin on Mary's resort, set up our tents in the yard (the bugs would have been too bad to sleep in the cabin itself), wolfed down our supper and continued to the Anahim Lake reserve. The large new indoor sports arena was full of spindly metal chairs—the kind with the moulded plywood seats—and about a hundred people, a large proportion of them residents of the reserve, were crowded upon them. (A similar meeting had been held in the Nimpo Lake Community Hall the day before.) Around the perimeter of the room stood at least a dozen RCMP officers, men and women: the Anahim Lake detachment boasts only four, so a large number had obviously been brought in for the occasion. Despite the heat of the evening and the stuffiness of the room, all of them wore bulky yellow vests loaded with pockets—were they flak jackets? If so, why? Who was going to shoot at them? But Stephanie said it was the pockets they needed: they wore them so they didn't have to carry handbags. There was also a guy with a TV video camera striding around, and a small, dark-haired woman carrying a microphone emblazoned with the CBC Radio logo.

The speaker, his voice distorted by his microphone and echoing hopelessly in the cavernous room, was almost impossible to understand. But he seemed to be distinguishing between an evacuation alert and an evacuation order. Evacuation alert meant that you should prepare to leave; an order meant that you were expected to get out of there. All the communities along Highway 20 from Kleena Kleene in the southeast to Stuie in the Bella Coola Valley in the west—including, of course, The Precipice—were under evacuation alert. Nimpo Lake and Anahim Lake were more or less in the middle. Nuk Tessli was now officially under an evacuation order, so we would have had to get out of there by the following day anyway.

"But do you really have to leave?" a member of the audience persisted. The speaker (another RCMP officer) was doing his best to keep things light. He explained to the man that he could not be forced to do anything, but should the order ever be given, it was in his best interests to remove himself. The man grasped the first part of the sentence and must have mumbled something about staying no matter what, to which the RCMP officer, thoroughly exasperated but still trying to make a joke of it, replied, "Then we will identify your body from your dental records."

The photograph on the front page of that day's *Vancouver Sun* had been taken at the Nimpo Lake meeting the day before. It portrayed a number of very fed-up-looking people, most of whom I knew. Among the residents was a woman with a hand over her face, apparently in despair. I heard later, however, that she was reacting to a similarly stupid question about evacuation with an "Oh my God I don't believe this" gesture. The photographer, however, had caught the moment and the picture expressed graphically what we were all going through.

The Charlotte Lake property owners were asked to stay behind after the meeting. Although Nuk Tessli was just as far from Charlotte Lake as was Nimpo Lake, I figured I was probably in that category, so drifted over to hear what was being said. The biggest complaint this community had was that in order to get reasonable insurance premiums after the terrible fire season that had affected other parts of British Columbia the previous year, they had armed themselves with sprinkler systems. Activated by a generator, these systems could operate several hundred metres from a water source and could run for 24 hours unattended. They were actually quite effective. To my amazement, I later learned that the Crazy Bear Lodge, already surrounded by flames as we had flown overhead, and another remote cabin on Little Charlotte Lake, where the flames had been tree-sized, had both been saved by such sprinklers. However, the systems could not function without fuel: if the people could not go back to their homes and cabins to gas up the generators, they were useless.

So far, although the fire had jumped the first cat road on the north side of Charlotte Lake and was still heading toward the community's properties, the other two firebreaks seemed to be holding. From now on, as long as the wind was not too strong, people would be allowed in for a maximum of three hours early in the mornings when the fire danger was usually less serious. This policy had a direct impact on us: it meant that we could go and pick up Stephanie Jane Hammond of Thunder Bay Ontario's car.

There are two roads into Charlotte Lake: the one servicing the settlement on the north shore, and another leading to the Forestry campground and the two part-time properties, near which anyone coming to Nuk Tessli on foot left their vehicles. Katherine stayed at Nimpo and walked the dogs (who were now relegated to chains and leads, so had to be specifically exercised) while I took Stephanie to her car.

The road to the Forestry campground used to be a slough full of enormous puddles and included a dramatic bog-hole through which you had to drive at breakneck speed, even in the driest times, if you hoped to get through. Extensive logging activities, however, have meant that culverts have been put in and there is now a veritable network of much wider roads throughout the whole area. As we got off the Hooch Lake Main, we were confronted by an RCMP roadblock. The young driver of the SUV took our names and warned us very seriously that if we were not out within three hours they would instigate a search and drag us out of there. I told him that all we were doing was picking up a car and as long as there were no mechanical problems we would likely be back in half that time. Why anyone would deliberately stay longer than they had to I could not imagine.

Smoke obliterated the sky, making the day seem very gloomy, but it was not all that thick at ground level. Visibility was moderate and the air was not particularly unpleasant to breathe. We picked the car up without incident and were soon back at the roadblock.

Standing beside the police vehicle was the man with the video camera who had been at the Anahim rec centre the previous evening. He let Stephanie's little town car drive by, but my old, dusty, rust-riddled Suburban must have looked more as if it was part of the landscape, and he stopped me and initiated a short interview. I asked him which channel he represented (there was nothing written on the camera). "Global TV," he said. I never watch television so had never heard of it. The situation was reciprocal, however—the reporter had never heard of me. I remember thinking, as I drove away, that I should have told the man he was on the wrong road—the north-shore residents turned off Highway 20 much closer to Nimpo Lake and there would be hardly anybody on this one. But I was already moving by then and did not have the energy to turn back.

Rosemary invited us down to The Precipice for a few days. Stephanie and Katherine still had a short time to spare before Stephanie had to fly out of Canada for her course, so I was pleased to be able to take them down to the Neads' wonderful little valley. Dave was away—in fact he was up at Anahim working as a fire coordinator. The Parks representative, Rosemary told me, was due to leave on vacation. Relations between the various government agencies, fire-suppression bosses and the community were very strained because of the slow response to the initial strike. Knowing of Dave's negotiation and facilitation skills, the Parks representative felt he would be the perfect choice to liaise between everyone concerned. Dave hadn't really wanted to leave The Precipice while it was under threat but felt he could provide this much-needed service. He was expected to be on call night and day so he was staying at the little Forestry trailer right in Anahim Lake. (Bizarrely, the notice board in front of the trailer, which indicated the level of fire danger, informed us that the risk was only moderate.)

We travelled on logging roads at first. As we descended the rough Precipice Valley track into the isolated valley, we drove out of the smoke. It was brilliantly sunny outside the pall and the sky was blue and clear. The afternoon turned briskly windy, and later we went to the top of the basalt cliffs that give The Precipice its name to see the fire clouds boiling up over the far ridge. Helicopter pads, back burns and cat activity had successfully blocked the fire on the north side of Trumpeter Mountain and The Precipice was no longer in such danger, though it was still well within the area of evacuation alert.

The fire was now making headlines all over the province, and news across the country and in the States. The smoke plume was fanning south and east, blocking out the sun in Vancouver, Seattle and for quite a distance into the Midwest. The fire was even featured on a satellite website that detailed weather disasters—alongside swirly hurricanes in Florida was the image of the long wedge of smoke with its apex emerging right from Lonesome Lake.

At six o'clock, Rosemary switched on the television to see what the Vancouver news channel had to say. The first person on the screen was me! I must have been the only fire victim to travel in front of that cameraman's lens. Later, many friends commented that they had seen the news clip. They had worried about me, but when they saw me, they at least knew that I was safe. The article in the *Province* had also been published that morning: "Well-known author will not leave her home unless she absolutely has to." But by the time the article was in print, I was already out of there.

The following morning I phoned Terry to see if he had been flying around to check on the fire. He had, but the smoke had been so copious in all the country east and south of the new flare-up, that he had been unable even to fly over it let alone determine what was going on. If we had still been home we would not only have been half-suffocated, we would also have been prevented from flying out of there even if we wanted to. So it was just as well that we had gone out when we did. For all that, I felt as trapped in The Precipice as I would have done at Nuk Tessli. The worry, the uncertainty and the inability to do anything about it made me feel as though I was going crazy.

When we drove back up the hill to Anahim, I managed to catch Dave in his trailer, and he presented me with a fire map of July 31 taken with an infrared camera. Neither the human eye nor ordinary film could have penetrated the smoke, but infrared sensors record heat and digitally transmit the information to the ground, where it can be printed out.

The fury of the fire when it really took off can best be understood by realizing that it took a month to get from the lightning strike to John's homestead near Lonesome Lake, a distance of perhaps 5 kilometres on the map, and two days to cover the 18 kilometres to reach Charlotte Lake. By July 31, the fire was stabilized at its northernmost tip, and on the north side of Trumpeter Mountain. The north and south sides of the Atnarko, and most of the west side of The Trench, were blocked by alpine areas. But it was still moving

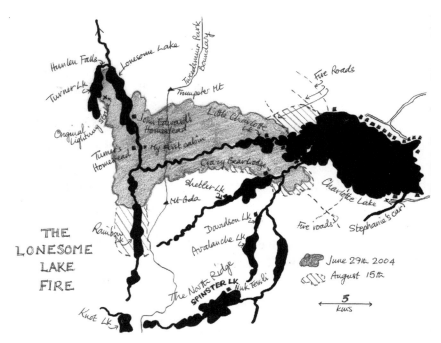

west at the southern tip of Turner Lake; south along The Trench; west along Crazy Bear Lake (which was in the valley immediately on the far side of the North Ridge from Nuk Tessli, but still a long way downriver); south along the Avalanche Lake valley, where it was heading straight toward my place; and southwest along the southern shore of Charlotte Lake. It was also hard against the second fire road on the north side of Charlotte Lake, but this was the area that was receiving the most attention: not only did the fire affect the Charlotte Lake settlement, but it was also directly upwind from the Nimpo Lake and Anahim Lake communities.

Work in that direction was of little help to my place, however. The moving fronts at Crazy Bear Lake, in the Avalanche Lake valley and The Trench were all creeping closer to Nuk Tessli. As soon as access was possible, a crew of forty firefighters was flown into the smoke blackened but still intact Crazy Bear Resort. The men would stay there a month, fighting fires in both that and the Avalanche Lake valley in an effort to save the other three or four remote cabins in that area, two of which belonged to Stewarts Lodge. These cabins were directly in between the fire and Nuk Tessli, so my home was therefore fairly well protected from that direction.

By far my biggest concern, however, was The Trench. I remembered well my attempts to hike through there, struggling through the horrendous swamps and windfalls, crawling through thick new growth and pushing my backpack through the branches in front of me. It would be impossible to fight the fire on the ground down there. The narrowness of the valley would seriously impede any retardant drops by fixed-wing aircraft, and the thermals generated by the precipitous valley walls would make life very difficult for a helicopter. What is more, cliffs act as chimneys: they cause major updrafts and exaggerate the power of a fire, often burning the country to the bone. A single day of strong north winds could bring this fire far enough south along The Trench to threaten both the valley to the north of me and my own.

Stephanie and Katherine, my wonderful wwoofers, headed off on their new adventure, and I prepared to wait, and hope, at the Nimpo cabin. The smoke wafted our way again and the dreary gloom descended once more. The Anahim Lake airport, where the firefighters were based, was only a few kilometres away, and from first light until long after sundown helicopters clattered back and forth through the smoke. Blood and bodies apart, it was just like being in a war zone.

The official figures given on the fire info website of the BC Forest Service showed that when John's place was burned, only 26 firefighters were on the scene, with no helicopters or heavy equipment. Four days later (when we flew out), there were still only 26 firefighters on the official records, but now 6 helicopters and 6 "heavy equipment" had been added to the firefighting effort. At that time, the fire covered 10,300 hectares and was 0 percent contained. The figures for July 31, a week after John had been burned out, indicated that the fire now covered 16,008 hectares and was 35 percent contained, and 300 firefighters, 14 helicopters and 31 heavy equipment were being used.

By August 2, a camp for 450 firefighters had been established. Anahim airport, which hosts the daily scheduled flights from Vancouver, is little more than a paved strip, a trailer for an office and waiting room, and three or four private hangars (one of which—where else but on the Chilcotin?—is built of logs). Now, the space between the buildings was jammed with trailers to provide meals, and rows of heavy army-style tents, portable showers and toilets. Several of the firefighters took advantage of such local accommodation as the area could offer—a dozen resorts and three motels—though much of that was already occupied by evacuees and the press. Soon, three or four helicopters were landing at Mary's resort each night. The locals, like me, had lost a great deal of tourist business, but most of them were now making more money on the firefighters than they would have done if the fire had never occurred. I asked Dave if he knew where I could apply for a job. I needed to offset all the money the fire was costing me—not just the lost tourist income, but also the expense of the emergency flight, and the food I was buying at Anahim at convenience store prices, when at home there were tons of supplies, purchased for the guests who would never come to eat it, just sitting there idle. I'd do anything, I told Dave: peeling potatoes would be fine. But the food crew had come intact; they needed nobody (and they probably used instant mashed potatoes anyway). Unlike other local residents I had no specific firefighting skills. One couple I knew, for instance, had been especially trained to be flown into areas where a fire had passed through. They monitored the situation, felled trees if necessary, maintained sprinklers and dealt with hot spots—dirty, smoky, dangerous work, but they were earning hundreds of dollars a day.

During my last days in the mountains, my website manager asked me for fire updates that he could post on his weblog. That led to an offer to put up a free newsletter for me on my own website. This was generous indeed, and the result, which was graced by the dramatic pictures Katherine took as we flew out, can still be seen there.

As with any other art form, writing is therapeutic in a traumatic situation, and putting down my thoughts at that time, whether for publication or not, was very beneficial for me. It also gave me something on which to focus my energies. I drew a map based on the infrared photo of July 31, extending the area to include Nuk Tessli, for my home was too far south to be on the official versions, and this was posted on my website as well.

By August 4, a week after I had abandoned Nuk Tessli, the BCFS website reported that the fire now covered 19,000 hectares, was 35 percent contained and employed 460 firefighters, 18 helicopters and 26 heavy equipment. The evacuation order, it informed us, was still in place.

On a helicopter ride around the fire zone, Dave Neads was able to take pictures of some of the salient areas. There was John's homestead, with its twisted metal and the bizarre patches of green juxtaposed with the empty black areas of ash. There were the Crazy Bear and Little Charlotte cabins, smoke-hazed but with a barrier of living trees around them, so amazingly protected by their sprinklers. Dave told me that my place would actually be in a good position to be saved this way, should the fire ever get that far. The buildings were on a squarish point, and it would be easy to run a sprinkler line to cut the point off. Moreover, a strong southwest wind like the one that had exploded the fire up the Atnarko (and which happened so often at Nuk Tessli) would tend to run the flames along the shore and might well bypass the buildings altogether. Should the wind be coming directly from the fire, it would arrive at the buildings after it had travelled over a couple of kilometres of water. This was always assuming that the wind stayed tidily in its dominant path and did not do crazy roller coasters and whirligigs, which unfortunately is the norm rather than the exception in the mountains. Nonetheless, this was of some consolation, but the smoky gloom of the sky matched the blackness in my soul, and my spirits were very low.

Dave has written many conservation-related articles for the local newspapers, and I avidly read his comments on firefighting in a piece entitled "Smoky Has Come a Long Way," published in the *Williams Lake Tribune*. He mentions that while the image of a firefighter with his watering can and shovel is still valid, there is a lot more to modern firefighting than that, particularly in such wild mountain country as ours.

As Dave explains, one of the biggest drivers of fire, wind, is extremely unpredictable in mountainous areas. The clouds often move one way while the ground wind does something completely different. I have often seen four winds blowing at once: three cloud layers moving in totally different directions, and a ground wind that bears no relationship to any of them. On top of this, a fire creates its own wind. The column of heat breaks through inversion layers, and it sucks air down to it, further oxygenating the blaze. Weather experts study these air flows on computer models and try to predict what is going to happen.

Ground fires are fuelled by fallen trees and duff; these move more slowly and can often be controlled by people with chainsaws and shovels. It is the crown fires that are the really dangerous ones. Contrary to popular belief, it is not dead standing timber that fuels these, but green, living trees. The oils and resins explode into flame all at once, sometimes with such force that the trees are vapourized, with not even a burnt stick left behind. Flames may reach hundreds of metres in height, and the vaporous fire clouds may climb to 5,000 metres. Under these circumstances, superheated air carries flaming material with it and drops it on untouched forest, thus sparking new burning areas.

Both helicopters and planes are used to dump fire retardant, which is a fertilizer mixture dyed red so that the pilots can see where it lands. The biggest chopper can lift 4,000 litres at once, the planes much more. But the planes have to come from the army base at Puntzi Lake in the centre of the Chilcotin. All their mechanics and equipment are based there so they must travel farther to get to the fire. They are also less mobile in this topographical violence, and their use is therefore limited.

Retardant can be very effective, but only for fairly small areas. Where the front of the fire is extensive, the only way to stop it is with a back burn, which is how the north slope of Trumpeter Mountain was controlled. This is a highly dangerous and tricky manoeuvre, and wind conditions have to be perfect. Sometimes the back burn is lit by ground crews with drip-torches, but for really large areas, two helicopters are used. The heavier one has the drip line on board. The pilot hovers above the target and presses a button that releases a flaming gasoline–jet fuel mixture onto the ground. The smaller bird-dog helicopter hovers just above the fire machine and gives directions to its operator, all the while watching for freak winds, smoke eruptions and other factors that may affect the safety of the men. As Dave writes, "To see these two machines moving in tandem against a black wall of smoke, dripping yellow fire into a forest, is like watching two huge dragonflies locked in a surrealistic mating ritual."

The August 5 edition of the *Coast Mountain News*, the weekly paper that serves the Bella Coola Valley, was naturally full of stories of the fire. John Edwards, Trudy Turner and Susan Turner all wrote long letters vilifying Parks, Forestry, the fire boss and the decision to let the fire burn. The paper does a nice little job for the valley, and Rosemary Smart, who flew in to Lonesome Lake before John had been forced out, was able to take a picture of John's current pet fox, Vicky, and syndicate it. Vicky, who was presumed lost in the flames, brought a sentimental accent to the grimness of the whole affair and appeared in a number of newspapers. So it was rather a shame that the August 5 edition of the *Coast Mountain News* just missed a development in the story. On August 4, firefighters dropped down to the remains of John's homestead to take a lunch break, and out of the forest, looking leaner but otherwise none the worse for wear, stepped Vicky. The excited firefighters fed her some sandwich meat; then followed a big panic to try to round up John. He had gone to ground in the little cabin he keeps in the Bella Coola Valley (like me, he uses this outside cabin as a storage/camping spot—his real home is in the mountains), and the cabin had no phone. But the following day, back he was flown, and both the *Globe and Mail* and the *Vancouver Sun* published pictures of John feeding Vicky. At

Vicky

once, John's future was clear. Until then he had had no idea where he would be living, but now he had a purpose. At least one of his family was alive and might very well need his help to stay that way. There was no decision he could make but to rebuild on the ashes of his old home. It was the first positive story to come out of the fire.

Up at Nimpo and Anahim, however, the uncertainty remained. Charlotte Lake residents were going into their cabins every day to refuel their sprinklers, but the evacuation order remained in place. Some rain was forecast. Would it be enough to make a difference? Nothing much in the way of precipitation fell at Nimpo, but the air turned cool and damp and dribbly, and on August 9, the evacuation order for the Charlotte Lake recreational area was (to use the official word) rescinded. The fire had grown to 19,812 hectares, BCFS maintained it was 80 percent contained, personnel were reduced to 245 and the equipment was downgraded to 13 helicopters and 5 heavy equipment.

I arranged to fly in first thing the following morning—but wouldn't you know it? The mountains were socked in with cloud! I was almost in despair. However, Duncan said he thought it was clear enough to take me in by late morning, and I drove myself and dogs to the float-plane base. Once again I forked out money from my dwindling resources to pay for the flight, and we were airborne and on our way back into the mountains.

CHAPTER 20

Business as Usual

Yesterday was cloudy and cool with a few dribbles of rain, and we heard that the Evacuation Order had been lifted for the Charlotte Lake community; an Evacuation Alert, however, would remain in place. I arranged for Tweedsmuir Air to fly me in first thing this morning . . . Everything here at Nuk Tessli is fine and it's back to business as usual.

—Report written for Jeffrey Newman's weblog,
August 10, 2004

I was actually quite surprised that Duncan thought it was clear enough to fly, for I could make out nothing through the wall of drizzly fog on the far side of Nimpo Lake. However, the pilot seemed to know where he was going, and we bumped off the water and drove straight into the greyness. Gradually, vague hill shapes emerged and it became apparent that the poor visibility was mainly local, caused by the smoke that still hung over Charlotte Lake; beyond that point, the air was quite clear.

Charlotte Lake looked very different from when I had last seen it. No flames now, and the solid-looking wall of smoke was no longer evident. But close to the ground, a wide swath of brown fumes streamed murkily from hundreds of spot fires both on the flanks of Trumpeter Mountain and along the south shore of the lake. This last area was deemed difficult to fight because of the ruggedness of the country (I had hiked through it many times; it would have been part of the trek to Charlotte Lake that I would have had to ski if I had gone out that way in the winter of 2003). It was indeed awkward: hummocky, rocky, peppered with swamps, littered with windfall, and consequently quite difficult to get through. The conflagration there was considered to be no great danger to anyone (where had I heard that before?) so was being allowed to burn unchecked. The burn was by no means complete; patches of green remained bright as flags amongst the blackened ash.

The shocking, sandy slash of a new road ran from the shore of Charlotte Lake to a rocky alpine hummock between the fire and the Forestry campground where Stephanie had left her car; presumably if this firebreak was threatened, more attention would be paid to the area. More fire roads cut through the bush between Crazy Bear and Shetler Lakes, and downriver from Davidson Lake, which was the one just below Avalanche Lake.

The forty firefighters were still camped at Crazy Bear Lodge working on these fronts. They had had to get the cat in, so the logging road that had originally been slated to cross Maydoe Creek just below Cowboy Lake, but which had never been finished thanks to a moratorium on logging in the Charlotte Alplands (largely engineered by Dave Neads), had now been punched through. Its scar lay across the landscape, straight as an arrow, a new man-made icon drawn upon the map. I was to cross it when I hiked out in September, and was stunned to find that it was as wide as a four-lane highway, composed mostly of smashed trees, but with a strong cat road along one side. It looked totally alien but was presumably unavoidable if we wanted to be protected from the fire. Apparently some four-wheeler operators had already gleefully explored this access into new territory and had pilfered fishing equipment and other articles from the abandoned and undefended resorts. People often ask me why I am so adamantly opposed to a road to my door, and this is one of the reasons. Once "civilization" reaches an area, nothing is safe. The Forest Service vowed to plow up key points along the roads to deactivate them, but they could not do this until all danger of fire had passed.

And so we crossed over the fire and flew along Davidson and

Avalanche Lakes, bumped over the small ridge that separates that valley from mine and dropped neatly onto the grey, wind-furred surface of my lake. But this was no longer an ominous grey; it was clean and rain-washed; there was a pearly freshness to the light and patches of blue were already peeping through the cloud cover.

It all looked so normal. There was no vestige of the fire here at all: no smoke in The Trench, none in the gap in the mountains toward Charlotte Lake, no burned patches, no helicopter noise. Usually when I leave the cabin I put all food and breakables in the attic, reasoning that they might be safer there from hungry bears, which has indeed been the case when they have broken in. But there had been no time to store the food properly when we evacuated. I had worried that the generous population of Lonesome Lake bears, who would surely have been displaced by the fire, would have found their way to my cabin and helped themselves. But there was not a trace of any animal activity whatsoever. Even my little gardens, which had been waterless for ten days in baking heat, still showed a few green leaves, though few of the plants were taller than 20 centimetres and most of them had bolted.

There would have been time for one of the parties that had cancelled to come in as planned, but faced with the uncertainty, the family had made other arrangements for that time. Everyone had been very generous regarding their deposits—only one group thought they might like at least part of it back, but in the end they decided to use it to book for the next year instead. Even the wwoofers I was supposed to have at this point had cancelled. They needed the security of having their feet under someone's table. All of which meant I was to be alone for a further seven days.

I took a hike up to the North Ridge to see how the flower meadows were doing, and they had pretty much fried. I also canoed up the lake to check on an eagles' nest. It is situated at the head of Spinster Lake, close to where the river runs into it. On the very smoky day that Stephanie and Katherine and the three clients had gone fishing, they had seen a half-grown bird flapping its wings while a parent brought food. I had first recorded the nest twelve years earlier and have seen a pair of adults hanging around it every summer, but had never before observed young. This, therefore, was interesting news indeed, and I wondered how the youngster had survived the terrible smoke. He was inactive that day, but I could see the top of his round brown head poking over the rim of the nest.

The fire, however, was still very fresh in my mind. As I always do when I am alone, I read a lot, and one book, a novel, described a family's flight from war. There was the frantic packing of possessions: the terrible indecision about what to take. My own situation, of course, was nothing compared to the horrors that a great many people have to put up with—I had health, I wasn't destitute and I had lost no one dear to me. I was in fact never worried about my own safety, only that of my possessions. What was all the fuss about? But it is the not-knowing that is the pivot of anxiety. And as I read about the fictional flight, my stomach clenched in sympathy and I relived my own feeling of helplessness during the evacuation.

There was a bit of thunder on the day I returned home, along with a very brief shower, but after that the weather turned hot and dry again. Winds were generally light and mostly from the south and southwest, but the fires above Shetler and Davidson Lakes continued to defy both the wind and the efforts of the firefighters and to creep inexorably toward me. The firefighters' camp at the Anahim airport had been downsized when the weather was damp, but now personnel and equipment were increased again.

Despite the prevailing wind coming from the opposite direction, the fire in The Trench was moving south. One afternoon a large plane, far bigger—and noisier—than the Vancouver–Anahim Lake scheduled flight (which often travelled overhead), prompted me to run out and see what was going on. It was driven by four turboprop engines and sported a very high tail. It was the retardant bomber from Puntzi Lake heading toward The Trench. It was bombing the timbered pass between Rainbow Lake and the next valley on the far side of the North Ridge: the fire must have been shooting up the steep side of the valley there. The plane made three trips in all, but that was it: either it was successful or there was simply nothing that it could do.

The shrinking of the snowfields on Monarch Mountain was another alarming result of the fire. Many of the snowfields had turned black, partly because they had thawed down to ancient ice and partly because of an overlay of soot. Glaciologists can take cores from ancient icefields and track the history of forest fires and other polluting phenomena: should any glaciers remain on Monarch in the future, they would record the Lonesome Lake fire just as surely as any computer. The darkness of the ice and snow would encourage an even greater meltdown. All mountain life has evolved to be dependent on the slow release of water throughout the summer from the permanent snowfields. Rain can never replace that water source, for no matter how much there is of it most of it runs straight down the mountainsides, and the minute it quits falling from the sky the ground dries out. This excessive loss of permanent snow is likely to have far-reaching consequences on the surrounding environment.

It was not long before smoke began to haze over the sky and turn the land masses back into murky cardboard shapes again. This time the smoke did not come from the Lonesome Lake fire, however, but from the Klinaklini in the south. This conflagration had never been restricted in any way, and as the heat and winds built up again, the fire clouds began to rear once more above the far side of the lake. The smoke hung in layers over Nuk Tessli, day after day, never as thickly as before but keeping Spinster Lake shrouded in various degrees of dullness and gloom. Some clients from Germany were visiting at this time, and they did not find the air smoky at all. For them, it was just like home.

The Berkés, the family from France who had been stranded for an extra day a year earlier, when the weather had been too bad to fly out, were planning a second visit. I had emailed them regarding the fire, but they had first heard about it when they arrived at the Toronto airport and were standing in line at the baggage carousel. A digital newsboard was listing world events: the Middle East situation, and so on—and suddenly, to their utter amazement, they saw the words "Lonesome Lake."

They decided to keep to their schedule and flew in on the morning of August 20. According to the weather websites for Puntzi Lake and Bella Coola, rain was forecast, but it had been promised before and nothing had come of it so I did not hold out much hope. I do not enjoy wet climates—I couldn't stand to live on the Coast—but I had never in my life wished so much for rain.

We did get a cloud cover that evening. As it grew dark, the red glow from the Klinaklini fire could be seen reflected on the cloud's underside. Through it, the paler, tighter fire cloud rose hundreds of metres into the sky.

August 21 dawned misty and dull, and then, unbelievably, it started to rain. Gently but steadily at first, it finally became a deluge that continued for 48 hours non-stop. Never before have I seen rain like that at Nuk Tessli. The ground was swimming in water and the temperature dropped 10 degrees. We were ecstatic—for all of the 48 hours. Then we were wishing that the damn stuff would quit. But the rain poured down for most of the following two weeks—more rain, I am sure, than we had had during the preceding two years. The poor Berkés. They had expected better weather than they had had the year before, but it was even worse. The rain was good news for the fire, however, at least temporarily. The rivers and creeks swelled, and the lake rose at least 40 centimetres. Now, from being at a record low all summer, it had reached a record high for so late in the year.

The fire, however, would not be completely defeated even by this biblical torrent. Duff and rotten logs would contain pockets of embers for months; they would probably not be extinguished until the snow fell. Should the weather turn hot and dry, the fires could flare up once again.

The fire crews were reduced, but the situation was strictly monitored. Fire season is generally reckoned to end in September, when nights are longer and cooler and there is less time for a blaze to erupt during the day. But when a Swiss wwoofer, who arrived a little sooner than the Berkés, left on September 7, she rode the bus out of Williams Lake beside a firefighter who had only just been let go. And it was not until several days later that fire season was finally declared over.

It stayed cool and rainy through the rest of the tourist season, but toward the end of September, when no one else was around to enjoy it, Nuk Tessli began to get some beautiful fall days. I canoed up the lake to check on the eagle. He (it was a small one, so probably male) was now habitually perched on a branch close to the nest, eyeing us curiously as I paddled by and the dogs ran along the shore underneath. Later I saw him flying effortlessly in circles over the canoe. A few puffs of smoke were obviously not going to make much difference to him.

On another occasion, I hiked up the North Ridge, as I always do before I have to leave and earn money in the big wide world. I like to try to plant the images in my mind so that I can carry them with me, although once I am out there I am usually too occupied with such concerns as getting squashed like a beetle on the freeway to think of them much.

This was a most glorious day. The tundra was orange-brown,

The eagles' nest

the sky blue, the air as clear as thin, new ice, the mountains dusted with clean, fresh snow and marching on and on into the distance.

The Mammaries would give me the views I sought, and I climbed first one peak and then the other, and looked down into the next valley. Patches of burned forest were visible both east and west. I could not see much of the valley bottom, and Crazy Bear Lake was hidden by a spur of land. But the forested slopes above it were blackened, and their edges were stained red with retardant. Looking the other way, I could see the upper part of the far wall of The Trench. The fire had travelled right up to the alpine on Migma Mountain (which is the one north of Monarch, and whose lower peak is visible from my window). It must have been very hot there and the forest must have been vapourized, for there was nothing to be seen on steep, fluted ridges but smooth, grey ash. I couldn't see very far down into The Trench, but I knew that the fire had burned right up against the pass leading into the valley that lay at my feet. That was where the retardant bombers were working the day they had flown overhead.

When I returned home I calculated these distances on the map. The Trench fire had come closest to Nuk Tessli: it had been quenched just 8 kilometres away.

Afterword

Many changes have occurred since I made that first chainsaw cut eighteen years ago, marking forever the virgin forest by the shores of Spinster Lake. One notable alteration is the official titles now given to the Charlotte Alplands and Whitton Lake (a.k.a. Spinster Lake). These designations appear on government documents and will eventually find their way onto maps. Another change is the increased use of the area by tourists. A local pilot once boasted that he may have been the first person to land an aircraft on Wilderness Lake; a year or two later a cabin was erected there, and now planes come and go all the time. Attitudes among tourism operators have changed, too. Instead of sneering at the "flower sniffers and tree huggers," they are now trying to adapt their businesses to attract them. This is not necessarily, I am sorry to say, evidence of a heightened environmental awareness but of economic interests. The huntin'-shootin'-fishin' crowd no longer provide enough income to support an outfitter, so they must turn to the summer people—the families, the photographers and the nature watchers—to keep their businesses going.

The trapping family who were the only real residents in the Charlotte Alplands when I first arrived no longer have much to do with the area. Trapping became uneconomical several years ago this far back in the woods, and when the family split, and the woman went to university and eventually back to the States, the father and son (the latter now in his twenties) let things slide. They still guided for the outfitter for a while, but they left their camps in a disgusting mess. Unconsumed store-bought food flown in for the tourists was simply abandoned. I always burned it if I came upon it before the bears found it, but it has made their campsites dangerous to be near. The last time I used one of them I was kept awake all night when my chained dogs barked continuously into the darkness—obviously at a bear. I was forced to sleep beside the firepit and keep the fire roaring all night—with the outfitter's wood—to keep the animal away. In the morning I came across the largest grizzly tracks I have ever seen.

One of the biggest changes that has occurred at Spinster Lake as far as I am concerned is communication. I started out with no phone of any kind: my only safety backup was to tell people when I was next expecting to arrive at Nimpo Lake to pick up mail—usually a month ahead—and to make sure I was always out on time. As the regular radio never worked during the daylight hours (and consequently I never listened to it during the summer), I did not always manage to keep track of the date but fortunately was never late enough that my absence initiated a search. After a while I acquired a single side-band radio, then upgraded to an FM Transceiver with four separate channels—all of which, with the exception of a local channel, rarely worked. For emergency communication the local channel was adequate and it stood me in good stead; the friends at the other end of the phone made up for any technical deficiencies. But it did not give me hands-on access to my business world, so finally I made the cyber-jump to high-speed satellite email.

The biggest change for me on a personal level is my physical fitness. When I arrived at Spinster Lake I was in my late thirties and had complete faith in my physical abilities. No matter how tough the task or exhausting the trail, I knew I could always keep going. Menopause put a stop to that. Now I realize my physical resources have limits, and I have had to learn to pace myself and expect to have put fewer kilometres under my belt at the end of the day.

This is nowhere more evident than in my hikes to and from the nearest road. Once I could do them in a single day, but now I always spend the night out somewhere along the trail, and I never attempt the difficult long winter journeys that even before used to require a good 24-hour recovery time. Not that I have to go out to Nimpo as much any more. The principal reason for those monthly trips was mail; and now I receive a lot more visitors by plane and the mail comes in with them. In any case, with access to the internet, my need for Canada Post's services has lessened.

I still hike to the road once or twice a year but now when I travel back and forth at all it is usually by plane. And this brings me to another difference between my earlier and later years here. In winter I used to be able to fly in by the middle of December and did not have to leave for spring work until late March or early April. Because of the milder winters, I am now lucky to be able to get in before New Year's and I have to leave by the middle of March. Because of changes in ownership of the air charter companies, and the accompanying sudden dearth of available winter aircraft, I may have to start looking for alternative winter accommodation.

The winter after the fire started a little earlier for a change, and by winter solstice there was already a reasonable amount of snow. Things were looking promising. I managed to twist someone's arm to put skis on his plane and was able to fly home on December 29. Once again we traced the route south over the plateau to Charlotte Lake and across the easternmost tongue of the Lonesome Lake fire. The burned and green areas were harder to distinguish: snow covered the ground between all of the trees, and the areas that contained bare, black poles did not stand out so much. The white *V* of the Atnarko arrowing down into The Trench looked pretty barren, though. The fire roads were white ribbons through the forest.

About 25 centimetres of snow lay on the ground around my cabins, which was actually quite good, more like what I would call a "normal" year. It was cold for a couple of weeks—down to –38°C some nights—but then it warmed up and it rained. It deluged for days and then rained for two more weeks, just as it had done after the fire. Nuk Tessli had experienced rain in January before, but never like this. When the clouds cleared enough to reveal the forest to the treeline, I could see that no snow lay on the branches there either, so it must have rained at a pretty high altitude. And in March it rained again. Another 24-hour steady downpour and several more days' thaw before it cooled off a little and froze again, at least at night. On the radio I heard speculation that it was going to be another dry year with another early fire season.

Apart from that, I had a good winter. I had to go out for a couple of weeks in February to take the first-aid course required for insurance purposes, but instead of going on a book tour in April and May, I gave myself the treat of staying here through breakup, something I have been able to do only once in all the years I have lived at Spinster Lake. I have to thank *Lonesome: Memoirs of a Wilderness Dog* for that. It jumped to the top of the BC Bestsellers list two weeks after it was issued in November and stayed in the top ten for one and a half years. The money I made from it during the fall book tour just about made up for what I lost because of the fire, so the bills got paid after all. I spent most of the winter working on three more manuscripts: the one you are reading, *Wildfire in the Wilderness*; a book on how to identify wildflowers for beginners; and an illustrated nature journal describing Nuk Tessli's year, for which I wrote the initial journal entries and made a few sketches.

Around the end of March, my wonderful new internet system refused to work. I had recently flown home after the first-aid course, and I phoned Rosemary and asked her to contact the pilot who brought me in to see if he was available. But due to the devastating March rain, he no longer had enough snow at Anahim to fly. The only way into my place, therefore, would be by helicopter, and I could not afford either to fly the equipment out or to transport a technician in. Fortunately I had copied all my business emails to Rosemary, and my summer guest bookings and fall slide-show engagements were pretty much organized, so I was able to sit back and let my good friend do all the work again. In May, when the ice went out, I took all the components—computer, modems and satellite arm—out with me. Apparently a small part on the end of the satellite arm had ceased to function: the replacement cost 60 dollars. But I had been without the internet for two and a half months.

During this time I had returned to the routine of putting my radiophone on at suppertime in case there was a message that needed my input before my weekly calls to Rosemary. Therefore, every Wednesday and Sunday I heard John Edwards' broadcasts from Lonesome Lake. During the previous fall he had flown in a pile of lumber and supplies, and he and four helpers erected a tiny cabin in which he has been able to spend the winter. He is slowly improving his dwelling, building a porch and so on. He has been feeding some squirrels, a couple of martens and his pet fox, Vicky.

Life, it seems, goes on.

Chris Czajkowski, (pronounced Tchaikovsky, like the composer), was born and grew up on the edge of a village in the north of England. Natural history always fascinated her, and she trained in agriculture, specifically the dairying industry. Once qualified, she travelled to Uganda where she taught at a farm school for a year. Chris then travelled widely through Asia, before arriving in New Zealand. There she worked primarily on commercial dairy farms and sheep stations. Chris spent her spare time exploring the beautiful scenery and discovering the flora and fauna of the region. It was in New Zealand that she first began to sell her watercolour paintings of the scenery and wildflowers.

After travelling through the South Pacific and South America, Chris emigrated to Canada. Attracted by the mountains of British Columbia, she eventually came to roost in an area of the Coast Range near Bella Coola, 500 kilometres north of Vancouver. She built a log house twenty-seven miles from the road and accessible only by foot and canoe. Through her letters to Peter Gzowski in the 1980's, she became a regular contributor to CBC's "Morningside" program. Her adventures during that time became the subject of her second book, *Cabin at Singing River* (Camden House, 1991).

Diary of a Wilderness Dweller is the story of her adventures building her second cabin, this time a mere 30-kilometre walk from a road. This cabin is located on a high-altitude, fly-in lake, from which she guides artists and naturalists on backpacking trips amidst the magnificent mountains that surround her. Living at such an altitude and so far from a road gives Chris a unique opportunity to study the wildlife in an area which has had so little documentation that much of it remains un-named.

Chris travels throughout British Columbia giving slide shows to local botanical and alpine garden clubs, libraries, and university audiences. She operates The Nuk Tessli Alpine Experience, an opportunity for artists, hikers and naturalists to discover the beauties of the Coast Range. She can be contacted by writing to The Nuk Tessli Alpine Experience, Nimpo Lake, British Columbia, V0L 1R0, Canada, or through www.nuktessli.ca.

PHOTO: YORK MEMBERY